# Three Man Game

## Surviving the Loss of a Wife and Mother

Jim Jarrell

*Three Man Game: Surviving the Loss of a Wife and Mother*
Jim Jarrell

ISBN 9780692906224
Library of Congress Control Number: 2017910363
White Oak Publishing: Charleston, WV

Published in the United States
Version 1.0
Printed by CreateSpace

Dedicated to Carol

# Contents

## Part Two: The Three of Us

# Preface

In September 2001, about eleven days after 9/11, I stood in a church in Pittsburgh, Pennsylvania, and watched my eldest son (of two) escort his new bride of three minutes from the church. This was "the girl" he had always wondered whether he would ever meet—the girl who was and is perfect for him. Just a few minutes earlier, as the ceremony began, my youngest son had delivered to the wedding guests a moving and memorable reminder of the victims of 9/11, from which the entire country was still reeling.

As my son and his bride made their way from the altar, he made eye contact with me. His nod to the organist in the loft was unnecessary. I had already recognized the recessional music to be "Ob-La-Di, Ob-La-Da," a track from the Beatles' White Album and which (on the surface at least) tells of Desmond and Molly Jones beginning a life together. It wasn't their best work, but it was simple, to the point, and certainly appropriate for the occasion.

I had been thinking all that day about how far the three of us had come after losing their mother and my wife to breast cancer in 1985. My son's choice of that "recessional hymn" was important not just because the three of us have always loved music (especially Beatles music), but because it signaled to me that my boys intended to be happy while honoring those years their mother and I raised them. As the reader will discover in the pages that follow, at times I had serious doubts about whether any of the three of us could be truly happy, given what we had endured. It has now been over thirty years since we lost Carol, the mother of my two sons and the first girl I ever truly loved.

I've never been bothered by round or big numbers like turning age forty or fifty. But for some reason, the roundness of the number thirty years in this case did bother me and bothers me still. My sons will tell you that it has rarely taken an anniversary to get me emotional about our loss—not just the loss itself but also the struggles we all had getting through various stages of life without her, the questions (especially in the first years) of how things might have been different had she survived, and the realization that we had finally learned to live with our loss in relatively good shape.

I suppose the preceding sentence ("the struggles" and "we finally learned to live with our loss") sums up one of the purposes of this writing—that is, it matters how folks face adversity such as a serious diagnosis (coupled with an extremely dire prognosis). And it matters in many ways. Also, even in the face of the loss of a loved one, there are ways to claw your way back to a productive and happy life. It sure as hell didn't feel like it for a long time, and it wasn't easy. But gradually, we did just that.

This is about the way we did those things. I'm sure there are many other ways—perhaps as many ways as there are people who face diagnoses and eventual tragedy. But maybe somebody can take something from this story of how we came through it all and put something of it to use in their own circumstance. That's reason enough for writing this book.

A more selfish reason is that I want my grandkids to know something of their grandmother. They'll never meet her. But to me, it's important that they know of her—who she was and is and how she reacted to and dealt with adversity—not just any adversity but one that was effectively a death sentence. I also want those kids to know from whom and where their fathers (my sons) came—both Carol and me.

Something happens as you get older and review a life that makes you more contemplative about people and events and their meanings. In my case, perhaps the single greatest meaning from our life struggle is the realization that my sons are now both well-adjusted young family men, capable of great things, and are men who will leave their mark on this earth. And I realize all that, even though I also know most of what we all missed from time to time by not having their mother around. Remembering where we started from when their mother was diagnosed and then when she died and seeing where they are now will always have an impact on me. Like I said, I suppose it's typical that the older you get, the more you are prone to look back upon life with some emotion. Kinda sucks—at least sometimes. At other times, it can be a good thing.

Having conceded that, I will say my emotions are less easily triggered these days than in the past. It sure isn't that I care any less. I just think it's all part of the process of learning to live with everything that happened, learning to live through tragedy, and frankly learning to enjoy (and rejoice in) the successes.

In any event, the thirty-year mark of Carol's passing in March 2015 compelled me to seek out something I had written some ten-plus years before,[1] in 2004–2005, and reread it. That consists of what is referred to here as part one, and I wrote it (although not fully aware at the time of my motive) more as therapy for myself than anything else. I wanted my sons to have a single touchstone to understand what their mother and I went through and how we tried to deal with it. I also wanted them to know our thinking behind how we tried to help them deal with the situation as children. As I wrote it, I realized that whatever its original purpose, the exercise was cathartic for me.

As I read in 2015 what I'd written over ten years before, three things struck me. First, I'd forgotten how clear some of the lessons I took from the experience were to me (and to Carol) then, as events unfolded in the years leading to Carol's passing and the few years afterward. For example, I was reminded of how quickly she and I learned the whole idea of

---

[1] The genesis and development of this piece are explained in the Introduction to Part One.

making the best of what one has to work with and living in the moment—an easily understood concept that is extraordinarily hard to put into practice consistently over time. Second, the story and (more importantly) the lessons I tried to take from it continue to remain relevant to me. In fact, it's been quite helpful to be reminded of some of those lessons and to apply them—or try to, at least—to my life today.

The third thought that occurred to me is obvious to anyone. It was that I had never addressed the second part of the story—how the boys and I managed over the twenty or thirty years following Carol's death as they grew into and reached full adulthood, setting out to create and live their own lives. I'll repeat: there must be an almost infinite number of ways to deal with tragedy in a healthy way. I don't mean to suggest that ours is the only or the preferred way—only that someone might find some of what we did useful.

So, I decided to pick this up again and add some things to it. But I didn't want to change very much of what I wrote in 2004–2005. Apart from a few minor edits, everything from part one (including the foreword and through the section titled "The Three of Us") is of 2004–2005 vintage. I'll refer to all of that as part one.

This preface and part two were started during the summer of 2015 and consist of general descriptions of different periods during that span of time, including a number of anecdotes (along with commentary—I'm rarely able to resist the urge to comment) illustrating various stages of our collective recovery from our loss.

The original idea of part two was that we would all contribute to the story, each adding his own memories and perspectives. But as I finished the first presentable draft, both sons were quite busy making their own lives and raising their own families. It didn't seem right to ask them to interrupt their lives merely to add their perspective to my own version of our story. Maybe one day they will add those perspectives for their kids or a larger audience. For now, I'm content to tell my story my way and hope that some folks can find within it something of value—something that might even help them deal with the prospect or reality of loss.

# Part One:
# The Four of Us

# Introduction

Beginning in 1985, I raised my two sons on my own. I had a lot of help from family. Their mother, the girl I fell in love with in high school, died of breast cancer less than two months before turning thirty-five. Our sons were nine and five.

The boys are now twenty-nine and twenty-five. Each in his own way is so much more than I could have hoped for even under the best of circumstances. As I write this, the elder is already a parent of his own little boy, and the younger will have his first son with him in less than a month.

Over the years, a lot of people have asked us how we managed—how we managed to rebuild our lives to a point where we could be happy; how the boys managed to develop into such fine young men, each with his own strengths and talents; how I managed to deal with my loss, raise the boys, and still handle a pretty demanding career; and just how we managed generally.

I'm never quite sure how to answer these questions except to say that you simply do the best you can with what you have to work with. In my case, I had a lot to work with in my sons. Frankly, to me the question isn't how I managed to raise them without their mother. Rather, it is "What would I ever have done without them?" The fact is, they were my salvation. They are the reason I didn't lose my mind or at least my way. They are the reason I learned to live with our loss to the point where I became content—a point I never thought I would reach. Eventually, much to my surprise, I became happy—at least in some basic way.

I will also say that I've become convinced over the years that great parents are made by great kids. I know of plenty of other parents who did at least as much as I did in terms of spending time with their children, setting the right example, and all the rest. Yet their kids made some wrong decisions, and the parents feel like they failed somehow.

Clearly, that view, while understandable, is wrongheaded. Though they take the blame for them, parents are not always responsible for the decisions their children make. In the majority of cases, I suspect that parents are rarely the principle reason their kids make bad decisions.

The flip side, of course, is that parents are not always responsible for the good decisions their kids make. All any of us as parents can do is raise our children with as much love and attention as we can, doing all those things we all know about— setting the right examples, enforcing discipline when necessary, instructing, and spending time with them in a variety of circumstances. The rest is up to them. All of them make mistakes and, if they're lucky, recover and carry on. Some make more serious mistakes and may not recover as quickly or as fully as others. But for the most part, those mistakes are the child's choice.

Again, great parents are most often made by great kids. I know that to be true in my case.

I suspect one reason I am asked so often how we managed to survive pretty much intact is because the boys and I have never shied away from talking about our experiences associated with their mother's struggle with cancer and her death. When we're together, we often reminisce about years past—although less so now than in the first ten years or so after Carol's passing. When we do talk, it's about all the things that happened during those years, both the good and the bad. People recognize that willingness to talk about it and I suppose feel somewhat comfortable asking us questions.

Our frequent conversations are what led my eldest daughter-in-law to suggest strongly one morning in my home that we should put our story on paper. She told us she enjoyed hearing stories about how the boys were raised and thought that some of the things we discovered in the process might be helpful to others. I'm sure the stories gave her much context in learning more about my oldest son, with whom she chose to spend the rest of her life.

So, here it is. I hope our story is helpful to someone—perhaps to folks who might be facing a struggle against disease, the loss of a dear loved one, or some other crisis which all too often intrudes into everyone's life.

Even if not terribly helpful, the process has been therapeutic for me. In fact, I suppose that's why I was never hesitant to talk about all this—even the unpleasant parts. It's always been therapeutic for me personally. I also suspect that when completed, I will realize that this project will have brought my sons and me even closer together—a result that by itself is fully worth the effort.

Jim Jarrell

# The Beginning

"It could be a carcinoma or sarcoma." I knew what those words meant. And here was this doctor who neither my wife, Carol, nor I had ever met telling me over the phone what he thought might be the cause of those "anomalies" he saw in Carol's blood work.[2]

I stayed calm for several reasons. First, I had to. Carol was close, only a few feet away—upstairs in our bedroom getting ready for bed—and certainly within earshot. Second, I am not by nature a pessimist. I knew that many cancers are treatable. Finally, I remember having the sense that this conversation had taken on an air of unreality. I guess in a way I just didn't believe what I was hearing. It just didn't seem possible that something this terribly serious could be happening to either of us. We were only thirty-one and had always been healthy.

It was a Friday night in late January 1982. Dr. Teller, an oncologist (I hadn't known exactly what an oncologist was until shortly after this phone call) had finally called at just after eleven. Carol had been dealing with back pain since early November. ("Honey, will you massage my back a little? I've got a kink in it that's really bothering me.") Given her back surgery some thirteen years earlier, plus the fact that she had a bad habit of carrying loads way too heavy for her small frame, we thought the problem was likely a muscle strain—or at worst, another disc problem.

The neurosurgeon who had removed her disc years before had reinforced our belief that the problem was structural (that

---

[2] To avoid unwelcome intrusions into his life, I have used a fictitious name for Carol's doctor throughout.

is, muscle strain or another disc gone bad). He admitted her to the hospital on December 1 after treating her for several weeks with various medications, primarily muscle relaxants. Those medicines continued in the hospital, along with physical therapy. None of the treatments worked. The pain simply got worse. It apparently never occurred to him that the problem might be something other than structural, even though he had available to him the same blood tests and x-rays that were to cause immediate concern in Dr. Teller less than three months later. He sent her home in mid-December to enjoy the holidays and said she should be fine with a little rest.

By mid-January, there had been no improvement. We had lost all faith in the neurosurgeon, so we went to our family practitioner. In addition to examining Carol, he reviewed the blood work and x-rays taken upon Carol's admission to the hospital at the beginning of December. He noted a couple of anomalies in some of the results and told us he wanted to call a specialist to review the test results. He said we should expect a call from him within a few days.

Well, here it was—the call we had been expecting. But we certainly didn't expect this tone, or words like "carcinoma" and "sarcoma" or his firm instruction to be at the hospital the next morning to be admitted for tests. After speaking with Dr. Teller, I chose not to repeat those terrible words to Carol. I merely told her he seemed concerned about what he saw in the x-rays and blood tests and he wanted to run tests in the hospital.

As she did with most things, Carol took this news in stride. But no one took the events of the next few days in stride.

That first day was filled with a series of tests, including a bone-marrow biopsy in which they inserted a needle into each of Carol's hips (her pelvic bones) with only a local anesthetic and extracted marrow from her hip bones. Dr. Teller told us there could be any number of explanations for the anomalies in Carol's earlier tests, including cancer. There it was—he had said it to both of us. Still, no reason to panic—let's just proceed and find out for sure what was going on.

Then came the bombshell. On Sunday, Dr. Teller sought me out, sat me down well away from Carol and everyone else, and confirmed our worst fears. Cancer. In fact, he said, over 80 percent of the material extracted from the bones in her hips was malignant. Prognosis? Two possibilities—both with the same terrible result. With chemotherapy, he said she might live as long as four to six months. But they would be hard months because of the toll chemo takes on the body. Quality of life— very low.

Second possibility—four to six weeks. And, for some reason, I remember very clearly him saying, "But I think I can get her in good-enough shape to go out to dinner with you and your sons." Yes, we had two boys, ages five and two.

My reaction? I honestly don't remember every aspect of it. A huge part of it was fear—fear of losing the girl I had loved since high school, fear of the future without her, fear for my two sons possibly growing up without their mother. Another huge part was anger. I suppose my first words were the product of both of those emotions combined. "Bullshit! I'll be goddamned if I'm gonna let this happen to her!" Now, I'm a good-sized fellow with a strong voice and reasonably assertive personality. And I wasn't at all restrained in demonstrating any of those attributes in this instance. Dr. Teller, a great guy, but still, a soft-spoken, slightly built Filipino, was obviously taken aback by that part of my reaction. But I think he realized most of what he saw was fear and not anger directed at him.

I'm sure there was more, but I couldn't begin to tell you exactly everything that went through my mind as it raced from one thought to another. Within a few minutes, though, I knew I had to go be with Carol. That meant I had to compose myself and suppress my emotions about what I knew. Further, Dr. Teller was suggesting (rightly, as it turned out) that we wait till the next day to tell Carol. That would give him a chance to further evaluate the tests, begin the process of getting a second opinion, and gather together all the resources available in and through the hospital to help us deal with the situation. (We learned early on that our hospital—a religious institution that had been around forever—had just equipped itself to deal with cancer patients on a long-term basis and that Carol was to be one of their first cases.)

The rest of that Sunday and the next morning were among the most difficult hours of my life to that point. As things turned out, they weren't to be the worst. We eventually lost Carol more than three years later, and I had to tell my sons, ages nine and five by then. Aside from the moment when I realized Carol was gone, telling those little boys was the absolute worst. And, of course, there was the job of "making it" without her—of raising our sons, of trying to achieve some level of contentment, if not happiness.

But it wasn't all bad, and no one should feel bad for my sons and me. The three years we fought for Carol's life were in many ways the best years we had together. And somehow, my sons and I learned to live with our loss. I think we learned some other things along the way that might be of some help or comfort to folks facing loss or the prospect of it.

Just about everyone at some time during life faces hardship in one form or another. We all wonder how we might do when it's our turn. My sons and I don't have all the answers, but through our time with their mother and after her passing, we found enough answers that worked well enough for us so that we each had a chance to be happy.

This is why I've put our story together—our hope that our experiences, with all the highs and lows, with all the mistakes, pain, sadness, tragedy, and all the rest, might help someone who reads it learn to deal with his or her own loss or hardship in his or her own way.

It's now over nineteen years since Carol passed away. Matt, our oldest son, is twenty-nine and a practicing attorney. Pax is twenty-four and studying psychology. We speak often of their mother—always have, even from the very beginning of our lives without her. Some of those who have witnessed those conversations (particularly my eldest daughter-in-law and the mother of my first grandchild) have encouraged us to write our story. We've never had to be encouraged to talk about Carol or about our struggle without her, so it didn't take much to convince us to collaborate in this effort. We hope it helps someone somehow.

# 1

# A Little History

Two American kids, doin' the best they can.
—John Cougar Mellencamp, "Jack and Diane"

Our story isn't particularly special to anyone else. But because we fell in love, got married, and had two great kids, it's very special to us. We had all the usual problems most young couples have—never enough money, uncertainty about the future and whether we could make it, among others. Like all couples, we had our share of arguments—some quite loud. After all, having married at age twenty-two (I was only two weeks older than Carol), we still had some growing up to do. But we were happy together.

I won't try to deal with all or even many of those cute stories that all couples have—those stories that demonstrate who we are, our weaknesses and shortcomings, our appeal, our humanity, and why we love each other. Just know that we have them and that we loved (and love) each other very much. But I will briefly relate enough of our history together to provide some idea of who we were, what we went through together, and what we meant to each other.

I remember knowing who Carol was and watching her as early as age ten or eleven. I was a pretty good basketball player in my younger days, and Carol was a cheerleader for one of the other teams in my grade school church league.

She wasn't the only girl I noticed back then—even at age ten, a boy learns to survey the field pretty early. But I do recall learning her name and watching her at those games. Little did I know then how important she was to become to me.

We didn't have much personal contact until we attended the same Catholic high school in our hometown as ninth graders. Even then, the contact wasn't anything special. Though I was attracted, there were no bells or whistles. I suppose you could say that she was in my "datable" group. I didn't classify girls consciously, but shallow though it may be, I think most kids at some level think of at least some members of the opposite sex as datable or not.

In any case, I found Carol quite attractive, though we didn't begin to make a serious connection until our sophomore and into our junior year. As a sophomore member of the varsity basketball team, I was tapped as coach of my homeroom girls' intramural basketball team. Carol was in my homeroom but absolutely refused to play. She was very self-conscious about her lack of athletic ability and certainly wasn't about to demonstrate that shortcoming, especially in front of me. But she did agree to be my assistant coach, a position that allowed us plenty of opportunity to engage in the verbal jousting that often passes for flirting between two awkward teenagers.

We began dating for real at the beginning of our senior year and continued into college, though we attended different schools. This was the period during which I came to know Carol as an intelligent, but somewhat shy, soft-spoken girl who could and would take a stand on any issue that was important to her. Her character was the most impressive thing about her. Plus, she shared my sense of humor—or seemed to. Maybe it was just to make me feel good that she laughed at most of my jokes.

Although she was a serious young woman, she was quite capable of doing or saying things occasionally that struck me as slightly ditzy. That may be too strong a word, but I can't think of a better one. One of the best examples of that was the time she and her mother attended a funeral of a woman who had known Carol since childhood. They did fine at the church.

But they realized after about five minutes at the grave site that they had found the wrong grave, the wrong funeral. They both realized their mistake at about the same time. They finally made their exit as gracefully as they could but not until after several minutes of giggling uncontrollably like two ten-year-old boys in church.

I think we both knew early on after we started dating that we'd struck gold. I don't think it was more than a couple of months into our courtship that I began to think of her in my life for the long-term. There was a brief period in our freshman year when I succumbed to the temptations that often confront basketball players at major universities (I had earned a basketball scholarship to the University of Kentucky). But I quickly came to my senses and worked hard to earn her trust again. Fortunately, she was very forgiving, and neither of us ever had any reason to mistrust again.

We married in August 1972 and spent the next year living in a mobile home in a college town. She worked as a high-school teacher while I attended graduate school. After I obtained my masters degree in public administration, we moved to the New York City area and spent a little over two years there. I had obtained my first real job with the Port Authority of New York and New Jersey as a management intern, and Carol worked for a bank in a town in New Jersey where we lived. At age twenty-three, we were both a little in awe of the glamour of me working in the World Trade Center and of us having the run of New York City in our spare time.

Our first son, Matt, was born in May 1975 in Rahway, New Jersey. By then, we knew two things. First, neither of us wanted to raise our family in the New York area. We simply weren't comfortable enough with the size of the area or with all the violence. I remember being so impressed (maybe "depressed" is a better word) with the fact that I had to watch the local news for a good ten to fifteen minutes before I heard about something other than murders and arsons. And, though we were never victims of any violence ourselves, we saw plenty of evidence all around us. We simply weren't used to it and didn't want to be.

I also knew from my experience with the Port Authority that I wanted to go to law school. But there was no way we could afford any of the schools in New York or New Jersey. So, we returned to our home state, where I took a job with the state government. The plan was for me to work there for a year to establish residency so I could qualify for in-state tuition and afford law school.

Like so many young couples, we struggled through law school. Carol returned to teaching English and social studies at a nearby high school, and I spent my time sitting in class, studying, or playing with our firstborn. Again, we lived in a small mobile home and often found ourselves searching the drawers, sofa cushions, and car seats for loose change so we could use at the grocery store or Wendy's. We were never in danger of starving—either set of parents would gladly have helped. But we went to great lengths to avoid asking for that help.

I graduated from law school in December 1978 and began working for a company in our hometown the next month. Carol stayed behind in our college town (about 150 miles away from my job) to finish out the school year in her teaching job. But we saw each other every weekend. In fact, it was during this period that Carol became pregnant with our second son, Pax.

After Carol finished her teaching stint in the spring of 1979, we moved into a house we had bought, and we began our typical American lives—family, home, jobs. Pax was born that fall, and the only thing missing was a little girl. So, we began in the summer and fall of 1981 to try for a girl. That was the first time we had ever planned for or tried to get pregnant.

That effort was interrupted in early November when Carol developed what we thought was a minor back problem. Carol simply sat in front of my chair as I was watching TV one evening and said her back was stiff and asked me to try to rub it out.

During the next few months, our lives were to change forever. The only potentially serious medical issue we had ever faced together occurred when our second son, Pax, was about six weeks old. I was at work one morning when Carol called me at about 11:00 a.m. telling me she thought something was wrong with our newest family addition. He'd been crying all morning—the kind of cry that suggested pain or discomfort of some sort. Carol had tried all she could think of to make him better but with no result. Knowing that I'd had two hernia operations as a kid and knowing what to look for, she checked Pax out and realized that she had likely found the source of the problem. So, she was calling me to tell me to meet her at the hospital where they were headed on doctor's instructions. Our family doctor was afraid the hernia had become incarcerated, meaning that the muscle may have shut off the blood supply to that part of the gut that had made its way into Pax's scrotum. That presented a potentially dangerous situation.

It was a little sobering to see this little six-week-old boy in pain and to know that someone was gonna cut into the little abdomen. We weren't scared by any means, but we were aware that any emergency surgery presents an element of risk. While we were waiting for Pax to be checked out at the hospital, I walked over to a water fountain while holding him, put some water in my hand, and baptized him.

We weren't particularly religious, but both of us were glad I did it. Carol cried softly I think because as routine as the surgery was, certain actions like that tend to bring the risks, however small, to a level of reality.

That experience was really nothing compared to what was to come in the next months.

The two months or so we spent working with the neurosurgeon were wasted. Carol showed no progress, and we still had no idea anything serious was amiss until our family doctor got what was to be Carol's oncologist involved.

# 2

# The First Days

After Dr. Teller told me about the cancer and what he thought the future held for Carol, he asked me not to tell her anything until the next day. He wanted a chance to gather his team together and make sure they were ready to deal with the situation in the way he wanted. The Catholic hospital he had admitted Carol to had just established a cancer-treatment program and did not typically deal with terminal cases. He wanted a chance to make sure everyone was ready. He also wanted a chance to tell Carol's parents.

He also wanted me to know before he told Carol. Clearly, he wanted me at least somewhat prepared to help Carol deal with the initial blow when he told her the diagnosis the next day. I do not recall whether I was present when Carol's parents were told. Nor do I remember specifically what their initial reaction was.

In any event, after Dr. Teller advised me of his findings, I spent the next hour or so grappling with the shock and getting myself (with Dr. Teller's help) under enough control to be with Carol without losing it.

I must say that during our ordeal, I developed an enormous amount of respect for Dr. Teller as a doctor and as a man. Aside from his technical proficiency, his ability to help us with the emotional and other more human aspects of our dilemma was amazing. He was always available for questions, never seemed rushed or impatient, and was always cognizant of preparing us emotionally for whatever was to come. He also understood and accepted my need to be familiar with the details of Carol's condition from time to time and to be involved in her treatment. Never did he let his ego get in the way when I would offer observations or suggestions. I will forever be grateful for his caring and compassion for both of us.

I returned to Carol's room determined to do my best to act as if all were normal but not at all confident in my ability to pull it off. We spent the next few hours watching TV, playing cards, talking about everyday things. She might have had a visitor or two. I don't remember.

Dr. Teller dropped by that evening to check on her and to tell us that test results from that day and the day before should be available the next day and that he would want to discuss those with us.

I suspect that Carol knew at some point during that day that something was amiss. She just knew me too well and was too smart not to notice some change in my demeanor. The numb, fearful feeling I had inside was overwhelming and (as I look back on things now) simply couldn't have been that well-hidden. I also remember noticing a difference in the way the hospital staff began to treat her. They seemed unsure of themselves and tentative—almost intimidated by her and her condition. But Carol didn't say anything to me or, as far as I know, anyone else.

The next day, Monday, Dr. Teller arranged a meeting in a conference room sometime around midday. He had his team of nurses, technicians, a social worker, and perhaps others. Carol's parents were also there.

This was the beginning of a pattern I noticed early on. When there was bad news to be conveyed, Dr. Teller was a master at creating a set of circumstances that would put virtually any reasonably intelligent patient on alert. That is, without saying anything directly, he would arrange things so that the nature of the news wasn't all that much of a surprise. That might sound like manipulation, and it is. But it was manipulation with a purpose—to allow the patient and those close to the patient to prepare on some level. And Dr. Teller was very good at it.

Almost as soon as Dr. Teller began to speak, I began to cry. I don't think I had cried at all since about age five. Again, I had this sense of unreality that it was all just too terrible to be real.

Carol noticed but never reacted strongly to my tears. She simply held my hand a bit tighter and listened to the doctor's diagnosis and prognosis. At some point, of course, she began to cry—but it wasn't a panicked, fearful cry. It was quiet and surprisingly controlled. She asked some questions, but I don't remember specifically what they were.

I do remember her initial response—delivered through her tears—to Dr. Teller's prognosis and recommendation. It was the only exception to the calmness with which she accepted the news. Recall that he thought (and he told her that day) he could keep her alive for four to six months with chemo, but that the quality of life would be so bad, he recommended letting the disease run its course while he managed the pain. That would give her about four to six weeks.

Carol's response, delivered through tears of anger more than shock and fear, was basically, "Wait a minute! I'm not even thirty-two years old. I have two little boys at home and a husband whom I love. And you're suggesting that I not fight! No way!" In Carol-speak, that meant "BULLSHIT!" Pretty emphatic and pretty tough. I was so proud of her.

Dr. Teller never argued with her. He simply accepted her reaction and assured us that he would do his part to help her fight. Then he told her that if she ever changed her mind, to let him know. That was the last time he ever spoke of anything but doing everything he possibly could to help Carol fight her fight in her own way.

Carol and I spent the remainder of the day in her room, simply holding each other, crying, and talking when we could. We comforted each other as best we could. Yes, she knew how afraid of losing her I was, and she did her best to help me deal with her illness. At least, that's the way it felt to me. Of course, her version had me mostly helping her. All that's pretty much what I guess one might expect from two people as concerned about the other as they are about themselves—if not more.

That night, I went home early enough to see my sons before they went to bed. Carol and I had talked about what to tell them, but only briefly. We both thought it was important to tell Matt (then age five) as much as he could understand. I don't think either of us ever thought of keeping them in the dark. Our main concern was in judging how much and what to tell them, given their ages. I didn't have to deal with Pax at this point. At just over two years old, he just needed to know that the doctor was taking care of Mom.

I told Matt that evening that his mom was sick—that she had cancer but the doctor was going to try to help her fight to get well again. Naturally, his first reaction was to ask if his mom was going to die. I knew that question was coming. I told him it was possible but nobody could tell right now what was going to happen. I simply assured him that his mom was OK at that point, that she was determined to fight to get well, and that she wanted to see him.

At the end of our conversation, he was concerned but not overly so. He seemed somewhat reassured knowing that he and his brother would get to see their mom the next day.

## Looking Back

As I look back on that day now, I think it was important to Carol for me to be open and uninhibited in showing my sadness, anger, fear, and other emotions. I guess I never thought that "being strong" for her meant hiding any part of myself or my thoughts. To me, it meant going through everything with her and helping her deal with all of it—all the tests, the treatments, the pain, the fears, the uncertainty—in a way that was consistent with her approach.

As it turned out, that day set the tone for the next thirty-eight months of Carol's ordeal. I never missed a chemo session or a major test—especially those that involved pain. I missed very few conversations with Dr. Teller and only one of any great significance (I will address that one conversation later).

My presence during those times wasn't just for Carol. God knows I wanted to do everything I could to help and support her. But it was for me as well. In fact, from the very beginning, I recognized at some level the therapeutic value to me of being with Carol every step of the way, of knowing everything that was going on and, as much as possible, what Dr. Teller was thinking about it. Aside from giving me a sense of contributing, it helped me to know what was going on, whether good or bad.

It also had another effect—one I never thought of until after Carol was gone and one that is almost entirely selfish. That is, after losing Carol, I never had any real question in my mind as to whether I could have done something differently that might have helped her more or made her last months significantly happier. I never had to regret not being there for her and wondering whether I might have made something easier for her. I guess I was convinced when all was said and done that I had done my best.

I also believe those first days were important for our sons, at least in terms of our setting the right tone. I never wanted either of them to look back with the sense that we were anything but as forthcoming and truthful as possible, given their ages. Obviously, that is a lot easier said than done. But we tried our best.

At some level, both Carol and I knew that whatever the outcome, what we were beginning to go through was a part of life. And tough as the truth is, kids can't be protected from that or any other aspect of life. I leave it to my sons to say whether we did the right things as far as they were and are concerned.

# 3
# Finding the Origin

We spent the next week going through a long series of various kinds of tests, dealing with the new challenge that had been thrust upon us and informing a few friends and folks at work of our situation. Dr. Teller quickly put Carol in an isolation room early on—one with only one bed. He required all visitors, nurses, and technicians to wear sterile masks and gowns. He did so for two reasons. First, Carol's white cell count was already depressed, rendering her susceptible to infection. Dr. Teller wanted to start chemotherapy as soon as possible. We knew that the chemo would depress her counts even further, raising the risk of infection even higher. Given the risks, we were happy to scrub and don sterile gowns and masks each time we entered her room.

Second, he wanted to give us more privacy than a semiprivate room would afford. We were still very much in shock and totally unaware of what to expect as the days passed. An isolation room provided a much better environment for all of us—Carol, her mother, and me—to deal with the situation.

As it turned out, only minimal effort was required to inform people about Carol's illness. Carol's mother and I learned quickly just how fast news travels. While we told a few close friends and relatives during the first few days, we began getting visits, calls, cards, and other contacts from a multitude of folks. Most were well-meaning, but we simply couldn't spend a whole lot of time dealing with all of them. None of them got to see Carol. Aside from the possibility of infection, we all knew she had to preserve her strength and focus. I suspect some thought we were rude or at least abrupt. But most appreciated what we were dealing with and simply delivered as much support as they could.

I had been with my company for just about three years at this point. But that made no difference at all. With very few exceptions among the ranks and file, they were understanding and supportive of my need to be with Carol as much as possible. I had been helping one of the more senior attorneys prepare for what was expected to be a lengthy hearing in Washington, DC, scheduled to begin in mid-February. Another attorney, a good friend of mine, was drafted to step in and take my place. I briefed him as best I could and stayed with Carol. My general counsel basically asked me to read as much work-related material as I felt comfortable reading, so he wouldn't have to charge my work absences against me. I couldn't have asked for better support from my friends at work during this period or those that were to follow.

Only a few of the tests were difficult or otherwise painful. Still, it hurt to watch her deal with them. What surprised me was their number. It seemed like a full-time job just to go through them all and keep them straight. Again, Dr. Teller was good at explaining to us, in language we could understand, what each test was, why he thought it was necessary, and what he hoped to learn from it, plus answering any questions we might have had. Difficult as they were to endure, knowing their purpose and importance made Carol's task of enduring them much more tolerable.

Generally, the purpose of the tests was twofold. First, Dr. Teller wanted to know just how far and where the disease had spread. As I understood it, that information might have influenced his treatment somewhat. But, more importantly, it might also have yielded some clue as to the second purpose of these tests—to find out where it had started. Knowing its point of origin would be important in determining what kinds of chemotherapy to use and how to use them.

From the beginning, Dr. Teller suspected breast cancer. His suspicion was confirmed after about ten days of tests when he performed exploratory surgery to examine the site he thought had been the start of it all—just between Carol's left breast and sternum. There had been no lump—no mass at all. Even when Dr. Teller examined the area after he thought it was the original site, he found nothing to suggest anything wrong.

This surgery confirmed his suspicion without a doubt. When he spoke with us afterward, he was very positive from the pathology report as well as his own observations that the disease had started in the breast. He quickly decided on the protocol of chemotherapy he thought would be best.

## Looking Back

I think there are two important aspects of this part of our ordeal. First, as bad as the news was, we had the sense for the first time since Carol's back pain appeared the previous November that we were doing something positive about the problem. Up to this point, we had little or no confidence that we had a good idea of what the problem was or that the treatments prescribed were the right response. In fact, as the weeks wore on with no overall improvement, what little confidence we may have had evaporated quickly and completely.

At least now we had a firm diagnosis and a plan for dealing with the situation. Though we were told that the prospects of success were not good, we knew what we were dealing with, we had our jobs to do, and we set about doing them. Our focus on those positive aspects of our dilemma helped our emotional states immeasurably.

Second, and at least as importantly, we were getting to know and like Carol's doctor. We learned to communicate effectively with him, despite the language and cultural differences. He always encouraged us to ask questions and never showed the least bit of hesitation in or impatience with any of our suggestions or observations. He made sure that we knew and understood why the tests he ordered were necessary, what they involved, what the test results were, and what those results meant in the overall scheme of things.

I cannot emphasize enough how important it was for us (not just Carol but for her parents and me) that Dr. Teller was so open and communicative with us. He seemed to realize intuitively that all of us had a need to be involved in Carol's treatment, and he accommodated that need very well. His approach formed a foundation of trust that was to be extremely important as time went on. Indeed, I daresay that our trust in Dr. Teller was one of the reasons we had the success we had.

Over the years, I have occasionally been asked to speak with people who have been confronted with a serious, life-threatening diagnosis, either in themselves or someone close to them. One of the first pieces of advice I always give is to make sure they choose a physician who they like and trust. I urge them to seek out a physician who will communicate as openly as possible and who will adjust the approach—not just the medical approach, but the method of dealing with the emotional needs of the victim and loved ones—to what the victim and loved ones need. This is what Dr. Teller did so well with us.

# 4

# The Battle Is Joined

Once the source and nature of the disease had been identified, Dr. Teller told us that this cancer was fast growing and that he wanted to be as aggressive as possible in dealing with it. But he also advised us that we would be walking a tightrope. That is, he wanted to give Carol as much chemo as he thought she could tolerate. But, given the fact that the chemo itself would inhibit Carol's ability to produce healthy blood components, he had to be careful to avoid rendering her body unable to function or to fight off infections.

As I recall now, he prescribed three chemo medicines and began to administer them only a few days after Carol's exploratory surgery. He worked hard at preparing us for the difficulty of the chemo treatments. We knew there would be periods of nausea and weakness. We knew Carol would likely feel jumpy and/or nervous.

As Dr. Teller began administering the first dose of chemo, I had a lengthy and important conversation with Carol. In effect, I told her to do what she needed to do without regard for my feelings or anyone else's. I wanted all her emotional energy and mental concentration to be focused on fighting the disease and getting better. I did not want her putting up with me or anyone else doing something—even something as simple as tapping a foot or asking her too many times if she needed anything—that annoyed her or distracted her in any way from her task. I told her to simply let me know as soon and as best she could what she wanted and when she wanted it. I promised that I would do my best to make it so.

This conversation took place over a period of a few days.

(My sons can tell you that I can be a bit repetitive at times). I viewed it then as part of our preparation for whatever was to come down the pike by way of challenges for her and us. It was the best way I could think of to help her—to let her take the lead in deciding how she wanted to deal with things and then to do everything I could to help her do it that way.

As that conversation developed, I began to bring her mother into it. Clearly, her mother was distraught. But she was and is a strong woman with a great ability to keep things in perspective even though her little girl was in deep trouble. She was going to be there almost as much as me, and that's the way we all wanted it. Plus, her mother has always had a refined sense of what her role should be in various situations, and this was no different. Though this was her child, she was glad to let me take the lead in helping Carol through what was to come. She knew I loved her daughter, and she trusted me enough to allow me to take on that role. I'll always appreciate that.

Carol received her first dose of the various chemo drugs without much incident or fanfare. She was fatigued quickly, but aside from that and a bit of nausea, she seemed to tolerate it pretty well. But Dr. Teller told us that the worst was yet to come. That is, we knew that the effect of the treatments on her ability to produce good blood would be a few days in coming. Sure enough, after a day or so, her blood counts began to decline significantly. The effect on Carol was quite significant too—much greater fatigue and the beginnings of mouth sores, making it difficult to eat or drink anything.

These first few days after the chemo consisted mainly of talking to Carol when she was able and wanted to talk, making sure we and everything or anyone we brought into the room was sterile (or at least clean), making sure she was as comfortable as possible while monitoring Carol's blood counts. In fact, the hospital staff, at Dr. Teller's instruction, allowed me unlimited access to Carol's chart and test results any time I wanted. The staff was uncomfortable with that arrangement. Clearly it was not the norm for them. But it gave me a real sense of participation in Carol's treatment. It also reinforced our trust in Dr. Teller.

The first cycle of chemo and the aftermath took about two weeks. We focused heavily on Carol's blood counts. We wanted them to increase as much as possible before the next dose, but we couldn't wait too long. Although we knew that the disease was depressed by the treatments, we knew it would be growing again and gaining strength in short order.

After a few days, her counts began to increase but only very slowly. It was soon apparent to us (though I'm sure Dr. Teller had known all along) that her counts would be nowhere near where they had begun by the time we had to start the second dose of chemo. Here was the tightrope Dr. Teller had warned us about. Wait too long, and the cancer gains ground. Administer the chemo too soon, and it might be too much for her body to tolerate.

The second dose of chemo hit Carol like a ton of bricks. As her blood counts declined precipitously, so did her energy level. The mouth sores returned with a vengeance, so eating, already an unpleasant experience, became almost intolerable.

This period of depressed blood counts, low energy, and extreme discomfort for Carol was among the most difficult periods we faced. Every blood test (and there were many of them) was important. We lived and died by their results. Though we did our best to encourage her to eat, she just couldn't. The nausea and mouth sores brought on by the chemo had made eating terribly painful. So, Dr. Teller expanded the range of intravenous nutritional supplements he had begun when her counts had started to decline.

The toll on Carol began to show dramatically during this period. Her color was bad. She was listless and at times not very lucid. And she had also retreated within herself—not in terms of giving up but rather in terms of concentrating on just dealing with the discomfort. In fact, I had the sense that she was purposefully directing her emotional and mental energy inward, as if concentrating on simply making it through the next hour or day put her one step closer to a goal—closer to being well again. I remember thinking that her emotional teeth were clenched with the effort of fighting through this terrible process.

We had a couple of scary events during this period of ten days to two weeks. The worst happened on a Friday afternoon. I had spent most of the morning with Carol but had run to the office to drop off some work and pick up some other things to do at the hospital. Carol's mother called me almost as soon as I walked into my office. The concern in her voice was immediately apparent. Shortly after I had left for the office, Carol had either sneezed or blown her nose and had started a nosebleed.

Now, a nosebleed is a minor event for almost anyone, unless that person had a seriously depressed platelet count. Platelets in our blood are an essential ingredient for clotting, and, despite several transfusions of platelets and red cells, Carol didn't have enough platelets to stop the bleeding on her own. Once that capillary in her nose broke, it kept bleeding.

The same thing had happened a few days before, and I had been successful in stopping the bleeding by applying pressure with an ice pack. Normally, the nursing staff would have handled the situation. But these nurses, much as they cared, seemed way too tentative to deal effectively with this situation. They were not willing to apply the degree of pressure I applied and were too concerned with Carol's protests about the cold ice. Believe me, I cared about my wife's comfort, but I cared much more about getting her bleeding stopped. Her blood volume and counts were already dangerously low.

I rushed back to the hospital that Friday afternoon, determined to work my magic again and stop that bleeding. But it didn't work. I spent a good two or three hours applying pressure. While the bleeding slowed, it never stopped. Dr. Teller arrived and almost immediately called in a specialist to cauterize the capillary—that is, essentially burn the capillaries shut to stop the bleeding. The process is very painful (we all know how sensitive the inside of our noses is). On top of that, the specialist had to pack Carol's nose with medicated gauze to keep the wound closed.

Over the next several hours, Carol's breathing became increasingly labored. Our concern was only heightened by the fact that Dr. Teller was worried as well. He told us that her blood counts and volume were so low that her body had to work much harder just to survive. She was in congestive heart failure—a condition in which the heart is too weak or blood supply just too little to supply her body's demands. He began blood transfusions as quickly as he could. Nevertheless, in short order, Carol's breathing evolved into "chain-stoking"— a heavily labored type of breathing in which the abdominal muscles do almost all the work.

By midevening, Carol's breathing had gotten even more labored, and she was not lucid at all. Her mother and I were very tense. One of the most helpless feelings in the world is knowing that things are going badly for a loved one and not being able to do anything about it except pray. And pray we did.

By about eleven that night, I asked Dr. Teller how long she could keep going like that. She had already been through so much and was obviously very weak. And now the very act of breathing seemed overwhelmingly difficult. Dr. Teller (like any other doctor) said he couldn't be sure, but he also said he would be surprised if she could survive any longer than about twelve more hours unless her condition improved markedly.

It's a fact of life that this world is filled with tragedy and that ours is not the only one. But this one was ours. At thirty-one years old, I was being told there was a good chance that the girl I had loved for years might die within a few hours.

Almost immediately I began to feel something akin to panic—a sense that events were totally out of my control. Worse yet, I couldn't even talk to the person I loved about it. I couldn't tell her all those things you want to say to someone who means so much. I knew I had told her those things before and that she knew I loved her, but for then that simply wasn't enough.

On the other hand, I had to be with her. I knew her mother would be present as well. Though she knew the situation was serious, she sure didn't need me showing signs of the panic I felt. So, I tried my best to discipline myself and spent the next hours with Carol and her mother, watching, praying, and hoping her breathing improved.

We sat and waited for hours. I think it must have been sometime around three or four in the morning that I thought I noticed some easing in Carol's breathing. I didn't say anything for fear that I might raise false hopes, but after another hour or so, I was sure there was some improvement. My hopes were confirmed by Carol's vital signs. Her respiration rate had slowed somewhat. And while her heart rate was still elevated, her blood pressure was increasing. Her color, which had faded dramatically, began to return. Everything seemed to suggest that her blood volume was improving.

By midmorning, it was clear that Carol was improving. She continued to get better throughout the day and during the days that followed. It was a long, tedious process, but Carol's counts bounced back remarkably well. She began to reacquire a healthy look, she became more alert, and she began to eat more and more.

We couldn't believe how well Carol did over the next two or three weeks. The improvement was steady in almost every way—her bloods counts improved, her strength began to return, and she was lucid almost all the time. After a week or so, she seemed virtually normal although somewhat weak physically. I began to relax a bit, especially after several of those moments of that slight ditziness I spoke of earlier that made Carol, Carol.

Finally, during the first week in March, almost a month and a half since she first entered the hospital, Dr. Teller began to talk about the possibility of sending her home. There were times after she entered the hospital when we doubted seriously if we would ever be having this kind of conversation. Of course, all this assumed that her counts would continue to improve. Dr. Teller wanted them to be as high as possible so that Carol would be able to fend off any infection and withstand the next dose of chemo.

On March 16, Carol's mother and I wheeled Carol out of the hospital and drove her home. I cannot begin to explain how good we felt. She was not supposed to have gotten to this point. We literally marched out of that hospital (well, her mom and I marched—Carol was in a wheelchair), knowing that plenty of nurses and other hospital folks had written Carol off long ago. Now, for the first time in a long time, we began to feel like we had a chance to beat this terrible disease. More importantly, Carol was so happy to be going home to be with me and our boys. It didn't matter that she wasn't in good-enough shape to even think about running the household. It didn't matter that she might have to reenter the hospital again after another week or so as the next dose of chemo began to depress her blood counts again. It was enough that she was going home.

One more aspect of this initial six weeks or so deserves discussion. With all our worry about Carol's situation and the stress of dealing with it, we were still the parents of two young boys who needed attention. Matt especially was old enough to realize that his mom was very sick. He was as vulnerable as anyone to being deprived of any news at all.

Carol and I spoke about them when she was able, and she kept telling me to be with them and pay them some attention. So, I made sure I saw and spoke with them almost every day, and I remember Matt coming to the hospital for a couple of visits with his mother. I don't remember much about those visits except that I tried to prepare Matt for the fact that his mother's appearance had changed significantly.

I'm still not sure what they were thinking during that time. I do know that we both worried about them and we tried our best, at least with Matt, to be as open and honest about what was going on without creating undue worry on his part.

## Looking Back

During this six-week period, we did what might be the single most important thing we ever did. For the most part, we got good at living in the present, at focusing on the moment and not letting ourselves, our emotions, and our perspective to be governed by the future. Though simple in concept and easy to understand, this approach to life is one of the most difficult to put into practice—especially when one is faced with potential tragedy. In my view, it deserves serious and constant attention by anyone facing any sort of challenge, especially one involving life and death. And it warrants some discussion here.

News of a terminal or potentially terminal disease is typically characterized as "devastating." I disagree with that characterization or, at least, I disagree that the long-term effect of such news should be devastation. That implies that there is little left of the victim and those close to the one afflicted with the disease (victims as well) to fight back with. If victims allow their circumstances and themselves to be so defined, it seems to me they're accepting that they are virtually powerless to change or even influence a prognosis—which, after all, is no more than someone's best guess as to what the future holds. To me, that gets too close to accepting defeat.

Even if that acceptance is limited to those close to the person afflicted, the odds of overcoming or proving a prognosis wrong are likely affected. Patients do not lose their perceptive abilities just because they've been diagnosed with a serious or terminal illness. They will likely discern that a loved one has given up at some level, and that can't be helpful. Not only must it be discouraging for the patient, but I also could see how it might even adversely affect the patient's level of trust in that loved one. I know Carol knew me well enough to tell if I had been anything but totally committed to helping her. We both saw others stepping back from loved ones in trouble. We were in a cancer center, after all. I shudder to think of how that might have affected our relationship or her ability to fight had she sensed that I was "writing her off" in any way.

Clearly, the news of such a disease is not easy to hear or to accept. And even I would agree that the first few days are naturally and unavoidably devastating to the victim and the victim's loved ones. The feeling of helplessness can be overwhelming. But once the diagnosis is digested, once the victims and loved ones have a chance to grieve and accept the reality, they have a choice. They can either accept the devastation and the prognosis, or they can choose to do whatever they can to defeat the disease and change the prognosis.

But what does it mean in real, everyday terms to fight a life-threatening disease and to avoid accepting a future outcome predicted by a physician? For us, it meant living in the moment focusing on the present much more than we ever had before.

It seems to be our nature as humans to worry and fret about the future, to know or think that something is likely to happen, and, in our minds at least, to treat that future as if it has already happened or to dread that possible future as if it is inevitable. This human tendency to let the past and a future (which, after all, has never existed) to define our present state of mind and our expectations of the future, I think, can be very limiting. In adopting that mind-set, we often forfeit the present. We fail to react to present circumstances, to enjoy the people around us or the simple fact that we are here with the opportunity to partake of whatever the present can offer. Worse yet, our focus on the future in this way often amounts to acceptance, even if implicit.

If we let that acceptance into our psyche, we not only forfeit the present but also forfeit to some extent the opportunity to change or influence that future.

Our tendency to accept a possible future is even greater

when that future is predicted by a doctor. Clearly, these men and women are held in great esteem by our culture—and for good reason. They deal in matters fundamental to our happiness, and those matters can be terribly complicated. They routinely take on life-and-death situations. Because of all that, they should be highly valued and admired.

But they are only human. They have no more ability than anyone else to "know" the future. In fact, most doctors will tell you just that. Many, especially those who deal with life-and-death situations routinely, will tell of events in which the future they predicted turned out to be totally wrong.

Believe me, I know it is much easier said than done to avoid total acceptance of a prognosis and decide to fight a disease like cancer. It's difficult for all the victims involved. But eventually, Carol and those of us close to her learned to do just that. We didn't deny the reality of the disease or the potential for an unhappy outcome. But we did make a clear and conscious distinction between reality (that is, the present) and several possible futures, none of which at that point were reality. We didn't deny that the odds were not in our favor, but neither did we accept the inevitability of those odds.

Essentially, we did two things. We consciously decided that the only reality was the past and present. We knew we couldn't change the past, but we could let it go and not worry so much about how we got to where we were. Obviously, we reviewed our past actions to determine whether we had done something to cause or contribute to Carol's disease. If we could have identified some past behavior as a contributing factor, we would clearly want to change that behavior. But aside from allowing the normal stresses of life (lack of money, raising two kids with both parents working, and so forth) to overtake us on occasion, we found no destructive behavior. Even if we had, it would have done no good and would have been counterproductive to have beaten ourselves up over it. Our ability to let go of the past allowed us to deal with our present circumstances much more effectively. Among other things, it permitted us to avoid that strange kind of madness that afflicts us all when, as we so often do, we worry about things we can't do anything about.

As to the present, we decided to make the most of it in two ways. Regardless of what the future held, we knew we had each other and our family at that moment, and we consciously chose to focus on and enjoy what we had then rather than let the future intrude and take our present away from us. Though simple in concept, this is not an easy thing to do. And we were by no means perfect at it. We all had our good and bad moments. But with lots of concentration and hard work, we got good at it—especially over the next three years or so after Carol left the hospital that first time.

Consequently, our state of mind was much better and healthier than ever before, and despite the circumstances we faced, we were happy most of the time.

The value of this healthier state of mind is hard to overstate. It not only rendered each day we had together more meaningful. It contributed to the sense I had after I lost Carol (and still maintain to this day) that we did everything we could in the best way we could. I absolutely know that she knew I loved her, that I would have done anything for her, and that I did my best to support her. Given the way things turned out, that knowledge is and has been invaluable. I've never had to look back in regret at something more I could have done but didn't or at mistakes I made (and I did make them). I just did the best I could (so did she), and that's all we could ever ask of ourselves or each other.

Also, we knew we could use our present to fight the disease—not just by taking the medications and chemotherapy prescribed by Dr. Teller and not just by making sure Carol didn't acquire some infection—but by using whatever emotional and mental energy we had to assist all of those other measures. This was particularly valuable during those first few weeks after the initial diagnosis and at other points when Carol's condition was not so good.

Now, I know this last part sounds a bit odd and maybe even new age-like. But we did talk in those terms. We knew we had to focus on the here and now to give ourselves the best chance for a future together. We didn't put the future out of mind entirely, but we did agree our best and most sane course of action was to keep our focus primarily in the moment. We tried our best to take things as they came, to enjoy each other and others when we could (even if the moment was a little sad), and not to let ourselves react to a future that hadn't happened yet.

Again, all this is much easier said than done. I do not claim that we always kept that focus. But we tried—and when one of us faltered, the others were usually there to help get things back in focus. Carol spent much of her time during critical periods being quiet and inwardly focused. I'm sure some of her silence was attributable to low energy and even pain. But I'm just as sure that much of it was due to her ability to be selfish and shut out everything going on around her so all her energy was focused on her disease.

I know my "preaching" over the last few pages about not accepting a future predicted in good faith by a well-meaning professional may seem narrow-sighted. Some people are clearly confronted with situations (medical or otherwise) that they can do nothing about. I don't mean that everyone should necessarily fight a clearly inevitable outcome. All I'm suggesting is that those folks be absolutely sure that the outcome is indeed inevitable and that fighting for a lost cause may simply be a waste of energy and time better used to some other end.

Even if the predicted results must be accepted, everyone still has it within them to determine how to face those results. The human spirit, when properly motivated and applied, is tremendously powerful, even in the face of ultimate defeat. Aside from whether society decides to allow one to end one's life in these circumstances, many of us can empathize with folks whose result is determined but who reserve the right to choose the time and manner of that end. I respect that choice and accept it as merely another expression or assertion of the human spirit. For Carol and me (and our allies in our battle), our choice was to fight to win—to prevail over the odds laid out by extremely capable and caring doctors.

I am convinced that our ability to maintain our balance most of the time enabled us to affect Carol's prognosis and our future from that point much more than anyone ever dreamed possible. It also made the three-plus years that were to follow the best years Carol and I ever had together.

At the beginning of that first six weeks when Carol started her chemo treatments, this ability to focus inwardly was extremely important. I remember telling (advising might be a better word) Carol early on that she should take the lead in deciding when she needed to focus inward—whether to practice visualization techniques (a process in which the patient visualizes the medicines attacking and killing cancer cells), to pray, to make sure she was properly focused on the real present versus a possibly unhappy future, or simply to deal with some discomfort and when to use her mother or me for things she needed, even if all she needed was a little distraction. I told her she should let us know what she needed and when she needed it—everything from food and water to quiet or some minor distraction.

Selfishness was not a natural part of Carol's makeup. But she knew what kind of battle this was, how much we all loved her, and that we were all willing to do whatever it took (and to do those things her way) to be of most help. Consequently, she was good at letting us know when she wanted something, when to talk to her, and when to shut up. And we got good at reading her as well.

These mind-sets provided a good foundation for this and subsequent periods in our battle. I don't mean to suggest that everything was calm, that we didn't go through some tough times, or that we didn't worry or cry or have moments of downright despair. And, after the initial two or three months and Carol's return home, we argued—that's what couples do. But we were always able to help ourselves and each other get back to these starting points so we were all pretty much on the same page.

Our approach seemed natural to me. But it apparently wasn't for everyone. In fact, a few of Carol's nurses expressed varying levels of interest in and curiosity about our ability as a group to hang in there together during some difficult times. I never quite understood why they were impressed—I just didn't see how anyone could approach things any differently.

One of the head nurses cleared it up for me. She told me that she and several of her nurses had seen loved ones begin to back away from patients almost immediately after receiving a terminal prognosis. She told me that more often than I would have believed, terminally diagnosed patients were left to deal with their situations alone—not in the sense that loved ones never spent time with them, but in the sense that they left virtually all care to the doctors and nurses. Worse yet, they distanced themselves emotionally from the patient, the very person they were supposed to love.

I can only say what seemed to work for us, and that was total involvement in Carol's care and realizing that there were certain emotional and other aspects of her care that we (and not the doctors or nurses) were best suited to help with.

# 5

# The Road Back

We were downright giddy as we left the hospital in mid-March. This was a departure that was not supposed to happen. At best, Carol was to have gotten only well enough to have dinner with me and our sons. No one expected us to be taking her home like this. But here we were, doing just that. As we wheeled her out of the hospital, her mother and I couldn't help but notice the looks we got from the staff. They were so happy for us. And I guess we were proud of ourselves and Carol too.

Happy as we were, we knew Carol was still sick. We knew she had to undergo many more doses of chemo and deal with the attendant nausea and jumpiness it causes. We also knew that she wasn't yet capable of running a household with two small children. Her mother and sister and my mother all pitched in to help. My mother, widowed for almost ten years by then, had watched the boys during Carol's stay in the hospital, and over the next few weeks, she generously continued to watch them along with Carol as I began to spend more and more time at my job.

Aside from the logistics involved in making sure Carol had the help she needed at home, our biggest issue during her first few weeks at home was in dealing with our sons. Though I had tried to see and spend some time with them nearly every day, Carol had been in the hospital. They had visited their mother a few times, but that time was anything but normal and nothing like we wanted it to be.

We wanted to get back to some semblance of normalcy as quickly as possible, but that was easier said than done under the circumstances. Carol was still not strong or energetic. Her time in the hospital—almost six weeks—had taken a toll on her, changing her appearance dramatically. The boys were not used to seeing her that way. And as she took her chemo doses every couple of weeks, she was even less capable of handling the boys alone until she got over the side effects.

At two, Pax seemed to be taking most things in stride. He was naturally less aware of his mother's condition except when it affected him directly. And she made every effort to be with him and have him on her lap when he would sit still long enough for that. I was able to give Pax more attention but never felt like it was enough. Nevertheless, at the time, he seemed relatively well adjusted to our situation and as reasonably content as any two-year-old would be.

Matt, at almost six, was another story. I've often said that Matt was born going on forty-five—he just seemed so serious about things and aware of what was happening around him. Don't get me wrong—he was a normal kid who had fun, sulked (or worse) when he didn't get his way, and was silly from time to time. But in addition to that, he always had this outward eye that was trying to figure out how the world works and what his response to it should be. Pax just wasn't old enough to do that.

As such, Matt had a clear understanding that his mother was ill and that it was serious. He knew she was weak and that the chemo made her weaker. He was also able to see the physical effects of the chemo on his mother. He had some understanding of death and the possibility that his mother might meet that end. But he also saw her improving over time.

I can't imagine what it must be like to know at that age that one of your parents—one of the two people closest to you and upon whom you depend the most for all kinds of things—is terribly ill. I remember thanking God at the time that kids have a natural defense mechanism built in to their psyches. They tend to be able to focus on themselves when necessary and can compartmentalize issues in their lives more easily than adults. But still, that ability is limited in any child—especially one with

Matt's outward orientation.

We decided we had to make sure he understood that Carol's improvement was good news, but that we still had a lot of work to do. We tried our best to explain everything to him as straightforwardly as we could, using language and concepts he could understand. In keeping with our earlier decision to be as honest and forthcoming as possible, we told him the essentials of everything we knew.

More importantly, we told him what we thought when he asked questions. And boy, did he ask questions. Any child faced with what we faced is going to ask questions. Those questions are going to take many forms, but they all boil down to essentially the same question. That is, "What do you think is going to happen?" Even kids want to know the same thing we all want to know in difficult situations. How is it going to turn out?

We made a conscious effort never to dodge his questions and to understand that he was going to ask the same questions several times. As to his desire to know what was going to happen, we simply told him we didn't know, we couldn't know, how things were going to turn out. We did tell him what we wanted to happen and how we were working to make those things happen. And we tried to involve both boys in that effort. He was grateful to be able to do anything to help, no matter how small. In fact, at that age there weren't very many things that were small to him. Anything he did was a big deal to him (and thus to us as well), especially after feeling so helpless when his mother was in the hospital.

From her arrival at home in mid-March to the next October, Carol improved steadily but gradually. She weathered the doses of chemo and their effects well, but clearly not without incident. She felt what any woman would feel when she lost her hair. One just cannot be fully prepared for the shock of awaking in the morning, looking back at your pillow, and seeing clumps of hair left behind. But she got a couple of wigs and fared well emotionally through all that.

And while her battle against the cancer was going well, the toll on her body brought about by the disease and then the chemo began to show. She began to gain weight and her back began to bow a little, the way an older person's back might bend under the strain of many years. Again, she reacted as anyone might—sad and maybe a little surprised and disappointed at the toll on her body.

As the summer progressed, though, her energy level rose after she recovered from each dose of chemo. She didn't have to be admitted to the hospital, though we returned there on an outpatient basis each couple of weeks to take the chemo.

Her mental and emotional state also improved markedly. In fact, we decided in June to get a new car. We needed one but probably would have put such a major purchase off because money was still tight. Though insurance had paid much of Carol's hospital bill, we knew we would be responsible for a small percentage of what turned out to be a pretty large series of bills. But our decision to buy the car was a statement: it said (to ourselves and to the world at large), "We are both going to be here for a long time, and we're going to act like it." It might not have been the wisest decision financially, but emotionally speaking, it did both of us a world of good.

She had begun to drive again in May and June, though neither her disease nor her treatment for it ever improved her ability—long suspect in my mind by then—to operate an automobile. She proved that in July when she wrecked the car we had had for just short of a month. I had been at work for just a couple of hours one morning when I got a call from a police officer in our hometown. He asked me if I had a wife named Carol and two sons. Just about the time I was sure something seriously bad had happened, he told me everyone was OK but that Carol had rear-ended a pick-up truck on the interstate.

My first reaction was to make sure no one was hurt. I knew how brittle Carol's bones were from the disease and how vulnerable she was from the chemo treatments. But the officer told me everyone was fine. My second reaction was to wonder how she managed to rear-end someone on an interstate.

I was greatly reassured when I got to her. She was obviously fine and so were the boys. Given that, the damage to our new car meant absolutely nothing. Now, that's an easy thing to say, but I mean it. I would have thought that damage to a new car would be at least slightly upsetting, even if everyone involved in the accident was OK. But that just wasn't the case. Yeah, I teased her about having several accidents, which tended to chew up our cars. But we were still so close to her initial life-and-death struggle that it truly meant nothing then.

Dr. Teller was nearly apoplectic about the accident. He knew better than anyone how fragile her bones were and how much damage could have been done if she had been jostled much harder. It was slightly funny to witness his reaction.

Funnier still was his reaction when Carol informed him that she wanted to take an aerobics class at the local YMCA. Here was this woman who had been deathly ill just two to three months before, who was still taking chemotherapy treatments, and who he had just chastised about taking too much physical jostling basically telling him she was going to take an aerobics class unless he forbade her to do so. He was certainly taken aback, but after a while and after extracting promises from her that she would follow his guidelines, he relented—and did so with some admiration for his patient.

She also became involved in the hospital's delivery of critical care to other patients. I'm not quite sure how it happened, but she spoke several times over the summer and fall with nurses, social workers, technicians, and some doctors about how she felt as a patient diagnosed with a terminal illness. She could tell them what worked and what didn't in terms of how various folks treated her, plus how much she and we needed to be involved in her treatment—not just in the decision making but in the treatment as well. I know that a couple of years later, they were still using the tapes of those meetings for new hires at the hospital.

Her improvement continued through the summer and into the fall. Her last chemo session was in early October. At that time, Dr. Teller advised us that he wanted to reassess Carol's condition by running several of the same tests he had performed the previous February. The most significant of these was the bone-marrow biopsy.

As always, Carol gritted her teeth and withstood the discomfort (doctors and nurses tend to speak in terms of "discomfort" or "pinches," but it's really pain) of these tests. We didn't hear anything for a few days and didn't expect to until we met with Dr. Teller. We were not terribly tense about what these tests would show. We knew Carol was much better, stronger, even approaching normal except for the lingering effects of the chemo on her body. These tests were just not something we fretted about.

All of this set me up for a surprise when I came home on a Friday evening in mid-October, walked into the kitchen where Carol was fixing dinner, and was told (with a pretty straight face) that Matt had something to tell me. I thought he had either gotten into trouble at school or had done something very good. He came running into the kitchen and, at his mother's urging, blurted out the news. "Mom's bone-marrow biopsy was clear!"

I looked at Carol, who by this time, was laughing and nodding her head "yes." Of course, I hugged her, and both of us were nearly crying (OK, we were crying) as Matt tried to hug us both. She told me that Dr. Teller had called because he was so excited and didn't want to wait until our appointment with him to tell us the news. He had not only found no cancer in the bone marrow, but he (and those who read such tests) also found no scar tissue either. He was absolutely amazed.

Of course, so were we. And we were also very grateful. We knew we had to be careful not to think the ordeal was over, but it was hard not to think we finally had the upper hand. When we met with him a few days later, Dr. Teller again expressed his amazement and his optimism for Carol's future.

He asked Carol if he could present her case to a medical conference of some sort in the Midwest. Of course, she agreed.

Finally, while he wanted us to enjoy our news, he also admonished us that he would have to keep watch over Carol for quite some time to come. He told us that diseased cells could still be in her body and we had to be sure to detect them, if possible, and kill them if we found them.

## Looking Back

One of the hardest things to do, I think, is to make the adjustment from living in constant crisis mode to living in normality, whatever that might be. After six weeks or so of such intense worrying about this test or that one, analyzing and discussing blood counts and what they might mean, being scared out of our minds by hemorrhages and congestive heart failure and then ecstatic twelve hours later by something as simple as regular breathing and an appetite—it's not all that easy to settle into a day-to-day routine in which one deals with mundane things like grocery shopping, laundry, helping kids with homework, and the like.

Yet we knew it was important that we do just that. It was important for Matt and Pax—especially given their ages. Both knew we were in a serious situation. Their mother's appearance and our honesty with them ensured that. But a young mind is simply not equipped to deal with continual crisis. (Frankly, I don't think anyone's mind is well equipped for that). Like all kids, they needed the stability and certainty of routine. We obviously wanted the best for our boys.

It was also important for us. It was a way of declaring, at least to some extent, victory over this insidious disease, which in our minds had almost taken on a persona. Having gotten out of the hospital and to a point where we could truly enjoy things day to day, none of which was supposed to happen, it was natural for us to reward ourselves a little bit by letting ourselves feel good about what we had accomplished.

Settling into more of a routine was also important for general health reasons. It's just hard to be anxious and filled with worry all the time, to wonder what news or downturn is just around the corner. The fatigue level for everyone—especially among Carol's support group—was very high. Now, I don't mean to imply that Carol wasn't tired as well. Certainly, she was. But it's a little bit like a parent being more nervous than the child when the child is involved in a big game. Carol could focus on how she felt, her state of mind, and getting through the various treatments and tests. She had to endure the physical toll that all those tests and treatments exacted. But she was focused on herself and on the moment. Because of some of those conscious decisions we had made early on, she got very good at keeping her focus limited in that way.

Our role was much broader. Our job was to focus on what Carol needed both physically and emotionally from time to time, to anticipate what those needs might be, and to ensure that those who encountered her acted consistently with those needs. We also focused heavily on her physical condition (it is hard to watch someone you love struggling to breathe or bleeding like an open faucet and not realize how much blood she was losing or what that could do to her), her tests, and what they meant. In short, we worried constantly—not always in a fretting sort of way—but rather, in a way calculated to enhance our ability to anticipate needs and events and to prepare her and ourselves to meet them.

I don't think it was until we had been home for a few weeks that Carol's mother and I allowed ourselves to breathe. I do remember a conversation between the two of us about the need to do just that. We realized that we needed to relax for our own sanity and health. More importantly, we realized that Carol needed the confidence that could only come by knowing we weren't always watching her out of the corners of our eyes, anticipating some serious downturn. She needed to become something other than the center of such intense attention and turn her attention to caring for me and her little boys.

As she made that transition, the effect on her was palpable. Her emotional state improved dramatically, and it seemed like the more normal she acted, the more normal she felt. She assumed her role as wife and mother gradually but with consistently increasing energy. She was good about not pushing herself too hard, and as we saw how well she handled things and regulated her activities, we became much more comfortable and relaxed.

# 6
# Back to Normal

By November or December, a mere eight or nine months after Carol nearly died that Friday night in the hospital, we were pretty much back to normal—at least in terms of our activities and Carol's role as wife and mother. She helped her mother with Thanksgiving dinner as usual. She did Christmas shopping for our family and decorated the house in anticipation of her favorite holiday. She helped Matt with his homework, played with Pax, and did all those things with the boys that a mother does.

We found it hard to believe that so much had happened over the previous twelve months. Starting with her backache in November of the prior year, her time in the hospital being treated for a muscle problem, the terror of the initial diagnosis, the hard work over the next six or seven weeks, the times we thought we were so close to losing Carol, the recovery that seemed too quick and good to be true—all that seemed so unreal twelve months after it started.

We continued this way into the next year and the following spring and summer (1983). Except for periodic visits with Dr. Teller (monthly at this point, as I recall) and taking a couple of long-term medications, the disease had little intrusion into our lives.

The boys enjoyed having their mother back every day— Matt especially. He was well aware of his mother's improvement. He realized at some level how good it was that his mother was once again in charge of the kitchen, the grocery shopping, and the household in general. He was delighted when she came out in the front yard that spring and summer to play whiffle ball with us, even though she was absolutely terrible at it.

Pax was happy too, although he was somewhat less aware of what his mother had been through. I remember him clearly enjoying being held by his mother at different times of the day. I also remember him being responsive to his mother's increasing role in his development. Carol's degree was in education, and she was particularly good at challenging both boys with different tasks designed to teach them social and other skills. Like any kid, Pax was eager to learn and responded well to his mother's efforts to teach. It brought home to me just how much he had missed her over the previous year.

As she recovered from the physical effects of fighting the disease for over a year, Carol was basically asymptomatic. She was energetic, she experienced none of the bone pain that had been so severe at the beginning of the ordeal, and her lab work was normal. Her hair had returned, but it wasn't the same hair she was used to. It had come in darker, thicker, and somewhat less fine than before—an odd change but one that Carol welcomed. She enjoyed her new hair with such different characteristics. Plus, she lost weight—she enjoyed that.

We went to the beach that summer with friends from my law-school days. They were the first people outside of family who I had called to tell them how sick Carol was at the beginning of 1982. We had a great time. Carol's energy and strength had returned almost completely, and she could enjoy everything about that vacation. She took charge of the kitchen when Matt, Pax, my friend, and I returned with a bucket full of crabs we had caught in the sound that separated the island we were on from the mainland. She was able to play with the boys and me in the surf—nothing too rough or demanding, but still, she played.

By the fall of 1983, it was almost as if nothing out of the ordinary had happened—at least on the surface. Except for our monthly visits to Dr. Teller, we were as engrossed as any young parents in raising our kids. Carol suffered very few ill effects

from the disease or the treatments for it and was even talking
about returning to work as a teacher.

We had even fallen back into our pattern of arguments. (I
think every couple has certain things they argue about, and we
were no different.) Rather than feel bad about those temporary
irritations, we embraced them. Well, "embrace" might be a
little strong. Let's just say we accepted them. We both felt that
the ability to express a little anger or frustration at each other
on occasion was just another measure of how far we had come.
She could see that I didn't feel like I had to treat her with kid
gloves (though I never did), and I knew that she knew I loved
her almost no matter what I said during these arguments. Sure,
there were limits, and we were aware of them, but we seemed
to have a somewhat better idea of where and what they were.
I guess what I'm trying to say is that, while we tried to avoid
arguments whenever possible, we weren't as prone to get upset
over a few words between us.

## Looking Back

These months after Carol's release from the hospital were
heady. We had been told that we would never again see days
like these; that Carol wouldn't survive any longer than a few
months at most; that our lives as we had known them were
over, although we had had no time to prepare ourselves for life
without her.

But we had beaten the odds. We didn't necessarily think we
were totally out of the woods, but we were a heck of a lot closer
than we could have expected at the beginning. And we were
enjoying it tremendously.

I think there were two reasons we were enjoying life so
much. The first is that we knew what we had and how precious
and fragile it was. And, by "it," I mean a lot of things—our
health (at least relatively speaking), each other, the boys, and a

life that was truly happy and fulfilling. It's true that you never fully appreciate what you have until it is taken away or at least threatened. And, like many concepts, it's easy to understand intellectually but difficult to make a part of your everyday life view unless you experience some real threat of loss.

But we had been taught that lesson by her disease and our struggle against it, and we were successful during this period in putting it to work for us in our daily lives. We tried our best to make this point with our sons, but at the same time, to avoid dwelling on the past. That would only have accentuated the risk that Carol still faced. Only Matt and Pax can say how successful we were in making the point.

The second reason we were so happy during this period was that early lesson of living in the moment. We were, for the most part, reasonably successful in not worrying too much about the future and not dwelling on the past. We didn't ignore those things—we took our lessons from the past. Carol spoke to others going through what she had been through. We also kept our eyes on the future—we never assumed as readily as before that either one of us was going to be around. But we were much less apt to be governed in our behavior or attitudes by the possibility of a future recurrence of the disease. Having been through some very difficult times, we felt we could handle difficulties going forward.

We didn't analyze our approach to life very much during this period. But we did have some conversations in which we were conscious of our ability to live in the moment rather than worry about the future or the past. I suppose that acknowledgment made us better at it and at being parents.

I have often remarked that these three years that Carol survived after her initial diagnosis were in many ways the best three years we ever had together. And that is true even of those parts of that time when she was ill. But these months when she was asymptomatic were the best. We got our lives back in pretty much every way imaginable.

The difference was, we knew so much better what we had.

And we knew it wouldn't last forever regardless of how Carol's disease progressed. Eventually, things would change. Our job, our opportunity, our only rational option was to enjoy that time as best we could.

# 7
# Here We Go Again

We made it through the 1983–1984 holiday season in great shape. Carol again did all her shopping, decorated the house, and helped put together a great Christmas and New Year celebration. But shortly after the holidays, Carol began complaining about headaches. They weren't terrible, but they were recurring.

I'm honestly not sure whether she told Dr. Teller or me about the headaches first. I do remember that he quickly ordered diagnostic tests. I also recall it didn't take him long to determine what the problem was.

He informed us sometime during January 1984 that Carol had several inoperable tumors or "lesions" in her brain. At that time, many of the available chemotherapy drugs were not able to get into the brain. As I understood it then, there is a filter of the blood that goes to the brain through which many substances, including some forms of chemo, cannot pass. That, of course, prevents the chemo from attacking any cancer cells that might have metastasized to the brain.

We were clearly disappointed and distressed. There wasn't the overwhelming panic that accompanied her first diagnosis, but we were very concerned. It seemed like we had just gotten things back to normal, and now we had a new challenge to deal with—not new, perhaps, but certainly somewhat different than before. Our initial thought was that we had beaten the disease back before, and we could do it again. Of course, there was the flip side of that coin: we wondered how many times we could get lucky and defy this insidious disease and the prognoses of experienced doctors. I was worried about the toll on Carol's body as well as her psyche. Despite our initial success, Carol's body had not escaped the ravages of chemotherapy. Just as important was her state of mind. It's hard to live with the constant battle for one's life, trying to act and be as normal as possible, while knowing there is a war in progress within your body and that its outcome means so much. I didn't know how much more she could take.

Though concerned and more than slightly disappointed that our earlier success was more limited than we had hoped, Carol's primary focus was on how we were going to treat this new development. She dreaded the thought of more chemotherapy and was not at all happy at the prospect of radiation treatments. But, as is the case in so many aspects of life, we and she had no choice. We had to do whatever was necessary to deal with the disease.

Dr. Teller advised us that radiation treatments could be effective, particularly on tumors in the brain. He also told us there was some chemo still available that had been found to be effective on brain tumors. His primary treatment was radiation. That meant Carol would have to contend again with bouts of nausea. She would lose her hair again. She would have to deal with weakness and fatigue. I don't know how she found the courage to do that, but she did.

Her treatments started quickly—well before January was over. They lasted for several weeks—into April, as I recall—and each seemed to affect her more than the last. Her nausea wasn't as bad, but with each treatment, she became weaker and more wrung out. I think we were both a little surprised at how much the radiation took out of her. I could see the effect of it on her body, even more so than the chemo almost two years before. She began to bow over more and more, as if her body was having trouble supporting its own weight.

Her energy level declined too. She was unable to do many of those household chores and things that she was so proud of resuming months before. I think the fact that her inability to run the household without lots of help affected (maybe "depressed" is a better word) her more than the grueling rigors of the radiation. I know she wanted to be in charge, to be the mom. More than that, I know how much she wanted to be a wife and mother to our boys and me in every respect. Her inability to do so hurt her deeply.

Carol spent a little time during this period in the hospital. Her blood counts (especially her white cell count) were low, and Dr. Teller wanted to be sure she didn't acquire any kind of infection. Although the reasons for the brief hospital stay were relatively benign, it still bothered me quite a bit. By this point, I hated the place and was frankly scared that one day Carol might go into the hospital and never come out again.

As if everything we had to deal with in the present wasn't enough to deal with, we encountered an echo from the beginning of our ordeal. There was still a balance of about $500 outstanding on the bill of the doctor who had treated Carol for muscle problems in late 1981. I had directed my company's insurance carrier not to pay it because I was convinced he had missed some obvious signs of the real problem in Carol's blood work and x-rays. His office had referred the matter to a collection agency, and they were sending increasingly nasty letters demanding payment.

I didn't involve Carol much in any of this except to tell her in a general way what had happened when it was over. I did involve Dr. Teller. I knew that he knew the offending doctor. I took him aside after one of his visits to Carol in the hospital and told him of the situation. I asked him to tell this so-called doctor that unless he called off his collections people and forgave the outstanding balance, I would make sure that as many people as I possibly could tell would know of his mistake. Recall, this was back in the day when malpractice lawsuits meant something—that is, they weren't assumed by most people to simply be attempts to extort money. In fact, I didn't even threaten to sue. I simply said I would make sure the facts of my wife's case, and his role in it, would be as widely known as I could make it. After a week or so, we never heard from that doctor or his collection agency again.

A few weeks after her first course of radiation, Dr. Teller conducted more diagnostic tests to determine how successful the treatments had been. He told us the tumors had been reduced in size by half. We had little idea what that meant. Was that the best we could hope for? Were more radiation treatments possible? Would the tumors continue to reduce in size even without additional radiation?

Dr. Teller told us that some additional radiation was possible, but he wanted to minimize it. He indicated there was such a thing as too much radiation—that is, there is a point at which it would likely do more damage than good. He told us that Carol's first course of radiation was heavy, but that additional radiation should be helpful. He also assured us that there were some chemotherapy drugs that might be effective on these tumors as well.

Though he sounded upbeat, both Carol and I came away from this conversation with the disturbing impression that he was at least somewhat disappointed with the results of this first course of radiation and concerned about the arsenal available to him going forward. We had both come to know and trust this kind and able man, and we could discern his apprehension. More importantly, we were open enough with each other that we could talk about our perceptions of his attitude.

We spent the next couple of months dealing with the additional radiation. Carol had had a few weeks (maybe even a month and a half or so) to recover from her first bout of radiation, so she was in relatively good shape. Still, the treatments took their toll as usual—nausea, fatigue, the rest of her hair went. But she seemed to hit a stride. Though difficult, it seemed to me that she tolerated these treatments well. Her headaches had dissipated, and her energy level was depressed but not as much as I would have expected.

She finished this second bout of radiation in September 1984. As the end of the summer approached, she had suggested that she and I get away by ourselves for a weekend—

something parents with young ones often talk about but don't often get to do. She wanted to go to a state park and rent a cabin for just the two of us. To say she "suggested" this weekend away is only half the story. Her suggestion became a strongly stated desire, which she turned into a reality. We reserved a cabin in the mountains for an October weekend at a state park she had visited often with her family as a kid.

Like any guy, I was more than happy at the prospect of spending a few days alone with the woman I love. But I was aware and slightly bothered by my sense that her insistence on this weekend had a sort of "now or never" feel to it. I didn't address it with her until we were at the cabin. She didn't deny that part of her motivation, but she assured me that she was as committed as ever to fighting and surviving her disease. Nevertheless, I detected a slight diminution in her level of conviction that she could overcome the odds once again. It was the first time I had ever detected even a hint of resignation in Carol, and that bothered me a lot. I feared I was beginning to get an answer to the question of how much Carol could take.

The reason for this sense that her confidence might be waning became clearer when we spoke about it again on the way home. We had had a great time during our few days alone but were eager to get back to our boys. She admitted she wanted to get away with me while she could. But not just because she thought she might not be here very long. She confirmed my suspicion that she was not feeling well in some serious way (that is, beyond feeling the effects of radiation treatments). She said she felt weaker and less energetic than she should. She knew (she probably said or meant "felt") that her discomfort probably meant more chemo, and she wanted to get a few days alone before she had to "go back to work."

## Looking Back

It can sometimes be hard to identify meaningful takeaways from a period that doesn't involve success, or at least a stalemate, in fighting against a disease like cancer. On the other hand, those might be the times when some things become even more meaningful.

Despite the discovery of the tumors in her brain, Carol maintained a generally positive outlook. Sure, there were tears and fear and a sense of futility at times. But for the most part, we kept busy with our lives to the extent we could. Part of her ability to do that was our conviction that this attitude was largely responsible for our earlier success and that, without it, we would likely find future success more difficult to come by.

Another part of it was our learned conviction that a forward-looking attitude simply made us happier. We had learned during the early days of the disease how important it was to have a positive attitude, to be looking forward and anticipating a future together. And we knew that whatever time either of us had here was best spent being (or at least trying to be) as happy as possible.

Having said all that, I don't want to mislead anyone about what our state of mind was. We worried about money (more specifically, the lack of it), our kids, Carol's disease, what the future held, and all those things that folks worry about. We had the usual arguments about everyday things—most often money—but also silly things like her putting my things somewhere and forgetting where I might find them. We had to deal with all those issues every other family dealt with.

But, underneath it all, we were happy. We recognized that life is not perfect, that it is usually messy, that there would always be annoying issues and problems we would have to deal with. But all these paled in comparison to what we had been through, and we knew it. In fact, we talked about it often. We talked about all our problems—but we also talked about everything that was right and good about our lives—our boys, the fact that we had enough money for food and shelter, our families, and each other. I think our habit of talking about all these things helped enormously in our efforts to maintain a healthy attitude.

Aside from shifting our focus to positive things, it helped minimize any damage recurring arguments can have between two people.

Carol had occasion to ensure her focus was where it needed to be during this period. Sometime in the spring or summer of 1984, I brought to her attention the issue of the doctor who had treated her for muscle strain when she first complained of pain in 1981. I told her that the same blood work and x-rays this doctor had supposedly seen led our family doctor, and subsequently Dr. Teller, to investigate the possibility of cancer. I told her that we might have a malpractice claim against him for having missed obvious warning signs and costing us several months of valuable time before we began addressing the real problem.

Carol's reaction was almost immediate. She said she had no idea how her illness was going to turn out and no idea how much time she might have left to her. But, however much time that was, she didn't want to spend it fighting over someone else's mistake. She knew a lawsuit would likely be contentious, and while this doctor should probably be called to task for his arrogance, she didn't see that as her job. In short, she decided not to pursue the matter based on what was good for her and us. It was truly an admirable decision.

We never spoke of the matter again. We did exactly what she had in mind—we forgot about exactly how we got to where we were, and we turned our attention to what mattered—getting Carol well again and enjoying our lives.

# 8
# The Final Battle

Just before Christmas of 1984, Carol began a new kind of chemotherapy designed to address the tumors in the brain. I don't honestly recall, but I believe Dr. Teller gave her a lesser dose than he would have if it weren't around the holidays. Still, the chemo had its usual effect and took its usual toll. Carol dealt with the nausea and fatigue and by Christmas, she was in good shape. We enjoyed our Christmas morning with the boys, saw both our families, and spent the next few days watching and sometimes helping the boys play with their new toys.

In January, Dr. Teller didn't hold back. He let us know that the situation was deteriorating quickly and, if Carol had any chance at all, it was to increase the chemo dosage to kill the cancer cells and try to deal with the consequences. He gave Carol the full dose of chemo and was going for maximum effect. The result was predictable—more severe nausea, greater fatigue, and, this time at least, very low blood counts. In fact, her counts were so low that she had to spend almost a week in the hospital. Talk about déjà vu. I didn't like this visit at all. That old fear that she would never get out rushed back into my consciousness. Although I tried not to show Carol my concern, I was more nervous during that visit than her condition warranted. I guess I knew how precarious her condition was and how quickly it could change.

Dr. Teller was concerned too. He delayed the next chemo treatment because Carol's blood counts took so long to recover from the earlier treatment.

Carol's next chemo was in late February. It hit her hard. As I recall, Dr. Teller knew it would and put her in the hospital before even giving it to her. He knew her counts would nose-dive, and they did just that. But this time, those counts were not recovering nearly as fast as they had before. In fact, they seemed to remain depressed for a long period. And Carol was in some distress. She was very weak and not always lucid.

At this point, Carol's mother and I became very worried. We knew we had to fight the disease for Carol to have a chance, and that meant chemotherapy, which was just so hard on her body in general and had such a dramatic effect on her blood chemistry. We all began wondering how much of this she could take. For Carol's part, she didn't seem quite as concerned as we were, and of course, we never made a point with her of the depth and extent of our feelings. She simply couldn't afford to be that worried, and I think she knew it. She didn't ignore her predicament, but she didn't dwell on it either.

Eventually, her counts did begin to recover. As they did, Carol's demeanor improved as well. She could read a bit, her mood improved, and she seemed to be returning to normal slowly but surely. I remember having a little argument with her one night. She had a bad habit that she was never to break of not recording checks she had written. As most families understand, that's the sort of thing that can make balancing a checkbook difficult. It's also something that can drive the spouse of the offender crazy.

That's exactly what I was trying to do (balance the checkbook) when I discovered one of her mistakes. In my frustration, I noted it to her. She shot back, and we had a few words. But as with most of our arguments, it was over quickly. Kisses and apologies were exchanged, and things were patched up quickly.

The difference with this argument, and the reason I remember it so well, is that it was the last one we were ever to have. One week to the day after that argument, Carol died. Her counts simply stopped improving, and she developed a condition called septicemia, which was described to me as an infection in her bloodstream. It affected virtually her entire system, including her brain. This was one of the consequences Dr. Teller had warned us about as a result of the higher dosage of chemo.

I won't go through the details of her last days, though I assure you I remember them all very well. I remember the increasing feeling of helplessness as Carol became less and less lucid, weaker and weaker as the septicemia spread through her body and made her condition worse. I remember her increasing pain and sensitivity to even being touched and Dr. Teller's increasing use of morphine to manage her pain. I remember the intensity with which I would question Dr. Teller and listen to and analyze his responses. I kept thinking that we had been close to death before and had recovered, so we should be able to do it again.

As Carol's condition deteriorated, Dr. Teller was forced to increase her morphine drip. The pain associated with septicemia can be horrible, and by just a few days after our last argument, Carol wasn't very lucid. The septicemia affected her brain, and the morphine kept her under. That was a blessing. The news regarding blood counts and other body chemistries just kept getting worse. It was clear she was losing ground.

She was moved to intensive care on a Sunday morning. I remember showering in the room she had just left and crying so hard. I guess I hadn't gotten much sleep over the preceding week and was scared about the direction of things. I had rarely been alone during that week, and when I was in the shower, I guess things just closed in on me. Even then, though, my attitude was that all was not lost. I still thought she/we could pull it off.

Later that evening, my brother was with me and seemed like he was ready to stay with me for as long as I needed him. It wasn't unusual for him to visit and to show his support, but I remember being conscious of the fact that it was unusual that he'd be there so deeply into the night. Also, Carol's mother left and went home. She had been at the hospital nearly as much as me, and I know she was absolutely wrung out.

It didn't dawn on me until later that evening, when a nurse who hadn't been very close to our situation tried in a pretty clumsy way to prepare me for the worst. I realized at that point that virtually everyone but me thought they knew where things were headed and that Carol was quite close to the end. Frankly, it pissed me off. I suppose I took it out on that nurse and a very thick and strong hospital window. The window wasn't damaged, but my fist was bruised for a week or two.

I forget exactly what this nurse's exact words to me were, but she was obviously trying to convince me to accept Carol's death as a given. But I knew Carol—I knew how strong she felt about fighting hard, how much she wanted to be with me and her sons, and how determined she could be when she wanted something badly. I also knew that Carol couldn't express any of her determination to us. Knowing all that, I couldn't give up and tell everyone to stop fighting. In fact, I never considered it.

More than any other time, I guess I considered myself her surrogate in terms of deciding how to fight and how long to fight. And knowing her and how she felt about never giving up, I simply didn't want to hear any message that suggested she had lost her battle. So, I simply reacted to attempts to get me to accept things on a purely emotional level.

I do remember asking Dr. Teller over and over whether she was in pain. Although I was willing to go through damn near anything to help her fight, I didn't want Carol to be in pain. He assured me that she was under very deeply and was not uncomfortable.

Carol's veins by this time were very nearly used up, but we still had to get medicine into her, and it was becoming difficult to do so. Because of that, Dr. Teller suggested inserting a port just under her skin at the top of her chest. He thought Carol was in good-enough condition to handle this relatively minor surgery.

I don't know if he was even able to start that surgery. It was about twenty to one on Monday morning, March 18, and I was waiting in the hall outside the ICU when a nurse came and asked me to come into the unit. When this very kind male nurse directed me to what I recall was a small supply room with Dr. Teller and a couple of other people in it, I knew the end had come. Dr. Teller told me that Carol had had a heart attack and that he had attempted to deal with it and revive her, but she had not responded.

I would have thought before then that I would simply have collapsed or gone crazy with anger or grief, but that didn't happen. I remember being calm and very sad. I assured Dr. Teller that both Carol and I knew how hard he had worked to save her, that we had been successful for at least some period, and that he had given us the best three years we had ever had together. I think that was the first time I used that phrase—"the best three years we ever had together"—but I would find myself using it repeatedly as the years passed. We hugged, and I was given a chance to spend time with Carol.

After about a half hour alone with Carol, I came out of her room and found my brother and Carol's dad there. Frankly, for the next several hours, I had this overwhelming sense of running on autopilot. It was almost like an out-of-body experience. To this day that's what I think of when I hear people describe themselves as emotionally numb.

I remember vaguely a few conversations. One was with her dad about his wanting to get her headstone; another was about how and when certain people should be told that Carol had died. I remember going to my brother's house—it must have been around two in the morning by then. My sister-in-law, one of Carol's best friends in the world and one of the nicest people I know, tried to feed me, but all I could take was a glass of milk. I remember how damned good that milk was—I'm sure it had been days since I had eaten anything—and how guilty I felt that it was good. I'm not sure what the psychology of that guilt was, unless it was simply that I was enjoying something and Carol was gone.

I laid on my brother's couch and think I did something that

might have passed for sleep for a couple of hours. When I woke, I was almost immediately consumed with a feeling of loss. As my mind cleared, I realized what had happened. Carol was gone. The boys and I were alone, and I was scared and lonely as hell, and there was nothing I could do about it. It was as if it had all just happened again. And, in a sense, it had. This realization that it wasn't all just a bad dream, that it had happened, was some psychological or conscious confirmation of the facts. In a way, it's as if I relived the loss as I became conscious in the morning.

What I didn't realize then was that first morning was to be repeated again and again for years to come. In those early days (the first several months at least), the intensity of that realization that I faced another day without her was quite strong. And it descended upon me every day upon waking. I think this accounts for a large part of the toll grief takes on a person. It's grueling and depleting. And it seems to go on for a long time. After a while and hopefully with as healthy an attitude as possible, the intensity of that feeling began to ease, but it was still there for a long time and improved only gradually.

On that first morning, added to that renewed sense of loss, there was something else—the realization that I would have to tell my boys their mother was gone. Funny (odd), I hadn't thought of that before.

## Looking Back

One of the most important things (I'm tempted to say "life lessons" here, but that seems too trite) that I carried away from this entire experience, and one of the things I hope my sons learned too, is the power and comfort of knowing you've done your best with whatever circumstances you're presented with—that you have done things and conducted yourself in a way that is consistent with who and what you are.

Note that I'm not saying that every act and decision must be "right" or the correct one in an absolute sense. But they do need to be the best thing for you and your loved ones under the circumstances. And that best thing is whatever is most consistent with your values, with what you know inwardly to be the right thing to do for yourself and the ones you love. This requires that decisions be consciously made.

It's not an easy thing to do. Many people (doctors, nurses, social workers, family, and friends) will make suggestions— some overt and some subtle and implicit. Some might even be unintentional. One needs to be aware, though, of what's going on and consciously make one's own decisions.

For Carol and me, this was a lesson we learned over time from the very beginning. From that moment when Carol told Dr. Teller that she couldn't just give up without a fight, she was making a decision based on what was right for her, based on what her own heart and soul were telling her to do.

Often when Carol was either not lucid, or so engaged in concentrating on her battle that no one wanted to disturb her unnecessarily, I had to make decisions based on what I knew of her and what I thought was right for her, me, and our boys. There were treatment alternatives (even if only elections of timing) that Dr. Teller presented me with from time to time.

Among the most important decisions I made were those during the last week of her struggle. These involved just how long we continued to fight and to some extent exactly how we carried out that fight.

I still have no idea whether every decision I made was the right one in an absolute sense. But what I do know is that I did my best. I made each decision consciously and with a view to what was best for her, above all. Only then did I consider anything else having to do with me or the boys.

The importance of this conscious decision making is difficult to overstate. And the result of doing it right can be profound. I've spoken to many people who have confronted crises in their lives—most, like ours, not of their own making. Some have resulted in the death of a loved one. Too often, some of these folks are disturbed years later by the decisions they made during the crisis. Some can't seem to find comfort even though they can't articulate anything they might have done better or even differently. Others seem to be haunted by decisions they made, still riddled with doubt about whether they did the right thing. That doubt can easily turn into guilt.

For my part—and I had this sense very early on after Carol died—I always looked back on what we did without any regret for anything we did as a couple, for anything I did in our relationship (except for perhaps losing my temper more quickly and thoroughly than was justified), or for any decision I made regarding her treatment. I cannot overstate the importance of the ability to live with myself and everything I did in these areas.

I know all that must sound somewhat arrogant and self-satisfied. So be it. I would much rather have this sense that I did everything I possibly could for the woman I love and take a little criticism for being arrogant than to constantly beat myself up for not having done my best.

# 9

# Breaking the News and Saying Good-Bye

I knew when I woke up early that Monday morning that I would have to tell the boys that their mother had died. I wanted to get home early so I would be there when they woke up to go to school. As I went upstairs, I had this terrible awareness of how much and how profoundly they were going to be affected by what I had to tell them—not only the immediate sadness and sense of loss but also during all those years ahead of growing up without their mother. Of course, my immediate concern was the need for the three of us to somehow deal with Carol's death.

I never had any thought of trying to hide my feelings, the sadness, the sense of loss, and even the fear. There was no way I could have done so anyway. Some who read this will understand from experience how deep and dark the sense of loss is when one loses a loved one—especially a spouse at such a young age. Even those whose understanding is merely conceptual can imagine how pervasive that sense of loss is, how scary it is to suddenly face a life without the one you love and depend on. No one could have approached the task of telling those little boys about their mother with anything approaching a calm or controlled demeanor.

I also never considered letting anyone else tell those boys what had happened. I don't recall anyone having offered, but I would have declined in any event. They were my sons. Their mother and I had been engaged as partners in the battles of life for almost fifteen years, and her battle against cancer spanned three of those years. We had made every effort to be honest and open with them, to involve them where possible without getting them so involved or engaged that it became harmful to them. Whether we struck the right balance in that sense is not for me to say. All I can say now is that is what we had been shooting for.

Matt woke up first. After he had been to the bathroom and was walking past the door to our bedroom, I called him in. I was sitting on the bed and knew that he very likely knew what I was about to tell him. He was a pretty smart and perceptive nine-year-old (almost ten) kid, and I was home in the morning for the first time in weeks. I know I must have looked like hell and had virtually no control over my emotions.

I did tell him. His response was natural enough. He started to cry and sat on my lap and hugged me. We didn't—*couldn't* is more accurate—say much after that, except that I tried to tell him we would be OK. I'm sure I couldn't have been convincing—I wasn't at all sure how we would be.

I told Matt he should go ask his brother to come see me on his way downstairs. Pax had been stirring in their room. At only five, Pax was less likely to figure out beforehand what I was about to tell him. But while he might not have guessed exactly what I would tell him, I think he probably knew something bad had happened. Matt had been crying when he told Pax to come see me, and I'm sure my appearance and emotional state must have been enough to alert him to the possibility of bad news of some sort.

As with Matt, I told Pax straightforwardly that his mother had died, that she loved us all and would always be with us in some form.

Pax had the same predictable reaction as Matt. But it was also a bit muted. And that was a healthy thing. I realized early on that kids have a built-in defense mechanism. Pax understood as well as any five-year-old could what had happened to his mother and what that meant for her and for us. And all that made him sad. But that understanding was not nearly as full or as deep as mine or even Matt's (there's a pretty significant difference between a nine-year-old and a five-year-old and their ability to understand this kind of event). Unlike Matt and me, my impression was that Pax didn't dwell so much on our entire future without his mother. He didn't quite understand at that point the love and emotional commitment between his mother and me, so he couldn't understand or appreciate the extent of my loss.

Interestingly, Pax's concern was probably the most selfless among the three of us. I'm no psychologist, but my thoughts are that his sense of self was not as developed as Matt's or mine, so his focus tended to be a bit more outward than Matt's or mine. He was immediately and thoroughly concerned for me. Natural enough—his big, strong dad was little more than a pile of mush that morning and for the next few days. His next area of worry was for his mother and her state of being. We are not religious people, but we are spiritual and believe in God and a hereafter. Naturally enough, Pax wanted to know where his mom was and whether she was OK and happy.

Early on, Pax's young age and the outward focus resulting from it was an advantage and maybe even healthy for him. It protected him from the tendency of those of us who were more mature and developed to try to deal with everything— our immediate grief and sense of loss, our future without Carol and all the rest—all at once (at least in our minds). Plus, it gave me some measure of comfort for his well-being. The little guy knew and understood what had happened and what it meant but only as a five-year-old could. There wasn't the tendency to look to the future as so profoundly altered from what had been expected or to think about what the absence of his mother would mean to him. That was left to the rest of us.

Although their reactions were predictable and healthy, telling those boys about their mother was absolutely the hardest thing I've ever done in my life. Losing their mother, the girl I loved, was hard, but as most parents will understand, your own pain somehow is more bearable than that of your children. I can't imagine having to do anything else in this life that hard again.

Those first few days were terrible. I was exhausted physically and emotionally and, of course, in a great deal of pain. Still, I was very concerned about the boys.

I announced that first morning, maybe three or four hours after I told the boys, that I was going to go see Carol's mother. She had left the hospital the afternoon or evening before, hours before Carol had passed, and I supposed it had dawned on me by then that she knew what the outcome was going to be. She and I had spent an awful lot of time over the past few years in Carol's hospital rooms helping to care for her, in our home when Carol was dealing with the effects of chemo, and at various medical facilities while Carol went through so many tests. I needed to touch base with her to make sure she was OK and to let her know that I was too.

Matt told me he wanted to go as well. I assured him he didn't have to. Frankly, I was a little worried about exposing him to so much sadness from so many people. I knew he cared about his mother, but I wanted him to have plenty of time to adjust to our new situation. But he insisted. It became clear to me that he not only wanted to go but, in a way, needed to go with me. He needed to face the situation more like I was trying to than how I might have expected from a nine-year-old boy. Plus, I think he wanted to simply be there for me—maybe out of some instinctive knowledge that his presence would indeed be of some help to me.

Whatever the reason in his head, I saw it then and still consider it an act of surprising maturity, which suggested a person of strong character emerging from this little boy. In the end, he went with me to visit his grandmother.

Pax had occasion to teach me a lesson about underestimating people as well just a day or so later. The night before his mother's funeral, I was putting them to bed. Of course, we were all still very sad. Pax asked me if he was going to have a chance to tell his mom good-bye. I told him that his mom was already gone. I forget his exact words, but he made it clear that he understood that Mom was with God, but he still needed to see her and tell her good-bye. He was emphatic.

I had already decided that Carol's casket would be closed. She had been through so much, and the chemo and other medicines had taken such a toll on her body that she didn't look like herself at the end. But Pax made me understand that this was something he needed to do. His request was made in such a way that I understood it was about him and his need, not me or Carol or anyone else. I was so proud of him for having the courage to speak up and let me know what he needed to do. And given his age of five years, I was a little surprised as well.

So, I called the funeral home and arranged to have her casket opened and waiting for us the next morning at our church. The three of us visited her one last time before she was buried. Pax did and said what he needed to do. Yet another tough thing to do—a part of the grieving process. Though hard, it was good for us. I think tangibly saying good-bye to the one who has died, as opposed to some "spirit," has value. And the whole episode taught me to listen with more than just my ears.

The funeral itself was later that day. It was simple and short. I'm sure the folks attending were struck by the tragedy of it all. The boys were fine, at least outwardly. I suppose we all looked fine. But of course, we weren't. We were lost, and it would take us quite a while to begin to see how we might manage. I suspect it might have taken longer for me to see that than the boys. They had the advantage of the optimism of youth. But I suppose I'd best let them address that issue for themselves.

## Looking Back

As I look back on that visit now, this time with Carol was a great moment for the three of us. We all had a chance to say our good-bye together. We talked to Carol; we spoke to each other and said good-bye as best we could. In a way, I guess I also think of that thirty-minute period as also a chance for Carol to send us off to face the rest of our lives, to lives without her there (at least physically). It's hard to overstate the importance of that last meeting, especially as time has passed.

In a broader sense, these first few days taught me something about my sons. Matt's matter-of-fact assumption that he would accompany me to visit Carol's mom and then his insistence on it struck me then and strikes me now as the kind of thing a man would do—a sign of a strong character in the making.

Pax taught me something about listening. We wouldn't have had that moment with Carol had I not been listening closely to my youngest son. Frankly, "listening" up to that point had been Carol's strength, not mine. Mind you, I wasn't out of touch with my sons, but at least until Carol got sick, I'm not sure I listened to them as well as I could have. Sure, I heard the words they said. But in this case, that last time with Carol would likely not have happened had Pax not been assertive enough to teach me to listen to the motivation behind and the intent underlying his words.

It's a unique moment in a man's life when he first sees signs of distinct individuality in his son's character, of the development of a stand-alone individual. Even during this terrible time of sorrow, I recognized what I was seeing in both of my boys. I tried to tell them that. I doubt I was very successful in doing so, but I've never forgotten that feeling of fatherhood, even if I couldn't enjoy it very much at the time.

# Part Two:
# The Three of Us

# 10
# The First Months

The first week or so after Carol passed was pretty much as one would expect. Many visitors and well-wishers tried to support us as best they could. My mom was always there, and my sisters—both of who were raising families of their own far from our town—visited to offer whatever support we needed. The funeral was not surprising in any way—sad with that overwhelming sense of loss. Anyone can imagine what we felt, so I won't attempt to describe it here.

Although those first days were challenging, the following days were even more so in some ways. It is simply a natural thing that, tragic as Carol's death was and as affected by it as people were, folks have their own lives. And the day comes when they must get back to those lives.

For me, that was a tough period. I knew the boys and I needed to find our own way without such a broad support system. True, my mom and Carol's folks were always there and ready to help whenever we needed them, and they were all there for years. But when the shouting is over and it's just you and the boys, there is a sense of being lost, of wondering, "What the hell do I do now?"

I suspect anyone who loses someone close goes through a similar letdown. There isn't a good answer. Perhaps the best I can offer is for people to be aware that sometimes support is best offered and most needed several weeks or even months after a loss occurs.

And I had to get back to work. My company employer had shown a great deal of compassion and understanding in allowing me the leeway to work as much as I could at Carol's bedside without penalty. Now, it was time to try to get back to normal. Much easier said than done.

The first thing I noticed at work was the kid gloves. Everyone's motives were pure, and there was no ill intent. But almost everyone treated me like a delicate piece of china that could break at any time. Even my male friends with whom I had shared a rough sense of humor were careful around me.

Much as I appreciated the intent, I hated the treatment. It made me self-conscious and aware that they were tiptoeing around me and my feelings. I found myself seeking out time with those who tended to be more direct about and respectful of my experience but didn't find it necessary to be too gentle. Eventually, most folks returned to normal, albeit at varying rates of speed. It was only after I approached "normal"—at least outwardly—that most folks settled back into their normal patterns. But that took quite a long time.

I say "almost everyone" returned to normal because there were some who could never quite get there. The best example I can recall was a secretary I worked with—very short and somewhat older than me, with something like six kids of her own. For a few years after we lost Carol, she would come into my office for one reason or another and occasionally focus on a photo of my two sons and simply break into tears. Not exactly what I needed. But how can anyone be too upset with such a heart, a heart with such uncontrollable empathy. So, although it could sometimes be distracting to me, I tolerated it, and before she retired, I even got to the point of teasing her a bit about her inability to control her emotions.

In contrast, my boss took a completely different approach—even in the early years. His conversations with me were appropriately sympathetic, but he never handled me with those kid gloves. Although caring for me and my sons, he always nudged me toward involving myself in pursuits other than raising the boys.

Just to illustrate the difference between him and others, I'll fast-forward for a moment to about three or four years after Carol died. That's when his approach reached a crescendo. He'd been encouraging me to "get out among 'em," by which he meant I should date women. I simply wasn't ready, but he kept prompting me—especially on one occasion when he was pushing a cute physical therapist he was using for rehab from surgery. In frustration, he simply bellowed loud enough for anyone on the same floor of our building to hear, "Lad, you just need to get laid!" He may have been right (or wrong). Even though I didn't act immediately on his suggestion, I appreciated the directness. He was a good guy with a big heart. What he said was funny, and he made me feel normal again for a while anyway. He always had that effect on me.

At home, things began changing almost immediately. My mom was in her sixties at the time. Nevertheless, she took the laboring oar in those early days of being there for the boys after school or taking them to her home for a time. I knew it was an imposition to ask a woman of that age to help, but I never had to ask explicitly. She simply did it.

Carol's parents (in their fifties) also helped immensely. They sometimes watched the boys after school, but they also took the boys in when my work took me out of town. Those trips were infrequent in the early years but increased dramatically after the first year or two. Those times the boys always felt comfortable, safe, and welcome with their Gran and Pop.

None of these people ever declined to help or complained. They all recognized the importance of me meeting my professional responsibilities and were happy to help—especially since they all loved my sons almost as much as me (not true, but I have to say that).

Two changes at home remain vivid to this day. First was Pax's need for physical contact. Even from his early years, Pax has been most like his mother—very caring and affectionate. I wouldn't call him soft by any means, but he is much more empathetic than his brother or me—and, back then at least, I think more needful of physical affection. Plus, between the ages of two (when his mother was diagnosed) and five (when she died), he spent precious little time in his mom's lap. So, his need to be in my (or someone's lap) was understandable.

He spent a lot of time in my lap or crawling through my legs as I tried to read the paper or watch TV in the evenings. I played with him a lot but needed time for myself occasionally too. It seemed to me he also needed a softness I couldn't provide. Later in the evenings, he would sometimes just curl up on my lap and close his eyes, but he never seemed comfortable there, no matter how hard I tried. So, I asked his grandmothers and aunts to do what they could to fill in the gaps. My thinking was that he needed a woman's softness. They all came through like champs.

I also noticed a change in the interactions between the boys and me—especially when it came to humor. No more than two or three months after we lost Carol, I noticed a "hardness" creeping into our treatment of one another. It wasn't meanness—it was more a lack of softness in the feel of our lives together. When we tried to exercise our humor with one another, it just seemed a little harsher than before. I suppose it was nothing more than just guys being guys, but it bothered me a bit. I never figured out how to deal with that issue. In the end, I guess it ended up not mattering so much.

There was another element of harshness that intruded too. I don't think it was there at first, but over time—probably a year or two—Matt and I began to treat the normal frictions between father and son with a certain edge. Eventually, it dawned on me. Before Carol died, even when the interaction was between Matt and me (two guys who were destined to butt heads more than a few times over the following years), her mere presence seemed to have a cushioning effect. It didn't always head off a confrontation. Matt had and has a strong personality, and I'm not exactly a shrinking violet myself. The result has been many frank and emphatic (read "loud" here) conversations over the years.

I never realized the extent of Carol's effect on the feel of our household at all until it wasn't there anymore. But when I did see it, it hit me like the proverbial ton of bricks. I tried to bring the softness back or at least set up circumstances that might accomplish the same end—time with grandmothers and aunts. I might have succeeded to some extent in minimizing this hardness, but there's only so much one can do.

## Looking Back

I can't begin to describe the fear I felt at the thought of raising those boys without Carol. There were other fears too, but this one was by far the greatest and is truly worth trying to articulate.

When one loses a spouse (even through divorce) that was expected to be there to help raise kids, the surviving spouse is (or at least I was) beset with an overwhelming fear that he or she is gonna screw it up. I loved my boys then just as I do now. But I was sure I was totally unprepared to raise them alone, even with the help of Carol's family and mine. I was equally sure that Carol would (in many ways) be a better parent to them than I could be. Of course, Carol saw it differently after her diagnosis. From the beginning, she always maintained that she would be better at dealing with cancer, whatever the outcome, and I would be better at raising the boys over the long term and by myself if necessary. She may have been right, but it sure didn't feel like it, especially just after we lost her.

The first thing I did was to continue in my refusal to hide my grief and pain from Matt and Pax. I'm sure I toned it down significantly for Pax, but I didn't shield him from the reality that his dad was hurting and would be for some time to come.

The next thing was to be sure I spent as much time with them as I could. I remember coming home from work and having dinner (usually prepared by my mom, sometimes Carol's). Instead of cleaning up afterward, I simply stacked dishes in the sink and dealt with them after the boys went to bed or the next day. The boys and I almost always found something to do (usually some form of baseball or basketball outside). We got quite good at inventing games in which Pax, despite the age difference, could be competitive. These games were to evolve as the boys grew older and stronger, and they became a major part of our lives together. More on that later.

I'm no neat freak, but I was brought up to clean up and do the dishes after meals. So this decision to stack the dishes for later was conscious and intentional. It was also one I never regretted, even though initially it slightly went against my grain.

It took a long time to get past that thought—that fear—that I was gonna screw up in raising my sons. In fact, I don't think a parent ever fully escapes that fear or the thought later on that maybe the parent should have done some things differently. I will concede, however, that my fear began to abate as Pax got into his late twenties, had a son of his own, and matured in ways that only children can bring about—with the help of his wife, of course.

Aside from the fear I felt in the immediate aftermath of our loss, our treatment at the hands of well-meaning people during those first few months left an important impression on me. To this day, whenever an acquaintance or relative loses someone, I usually try to find a gentle way to prepare that person for that time when many of the supporters return to their own lives and the ones left standing are expected to piece their lives together somehow without the person lost. By no means am I being judgmental about those returning to their own lives. They have their lives and that includes other people depending on them. My sisters had husbands and kids of their own. Same with Carol's siblings. It's perfectly natural that they return to their lives and carry on. But those closest to the deceased will always find it hard after the first two or three weeks to begin the task of rebuilding their lives after the initial support group begins to return to their own lives. It's a lonely task, and there's little anyone can do to make it easier. I simply have tried to make it a practice to offer an ear to talk to. But it wasn't enough for me to offer once or twice. I would make the offer maybe two weeks after a funeral and again after a month, and then again after two months—again even after a year or two. You never know when that offer might come at just the right time for that person. And I learned that it simply isn't in many people's nature to make the contact or to ask for that ear to talk to or shoulder to cry on. Sometimes you have to risk becoming a pest and chase the opportunity down to help over time.

If you are lucky enough to have someone grieving open up to you, be honest and direct. Bromides and platitudes are generally not helpful. Among the most effective and helpful people I spoke to were those who were sympathetic, maybe even empathetic, without allowing me to wallow in my grief. Yeah, some tears and expression of despair early on are quite natural. But my brother's admonition about a month after Carol passed to "get on with it" was a helpful (if somewhat shocking in the moment) splash of ice-cold water in my face. He helped me realize I had a job to do for my boys and for myself, and it wasn't going to help anything or anyone to spend my life grieving.

Speaking of bromides, I will admit that some do find comfort in attributing bad events to God's will. I'm not among them. That is, I don't think God sits and decides this one goes and this one stays with loved ones. It seems more likely to me that we're all put down here in something akin to a big pinball machine, and no one knows or plans out what's going to happen. But we all know bad—and good—things will happen to us all. It seems more likely to me that our test is how we handle those things—both the good and the bad. Maybe that was just my way of avoiding a life full of anger at a deity I'm not positive even exists, but I do remember going through that thought process after Carol's diagnosis and even more so after we lost her.

# 11
# The First Years

The first two years without Carol were tough. I spent most of that time trying to adjust to life without her and worrying a lot about my sons and whether I was doing right by them. Let me take those things in order.

That first year is full of firsts. The first Easter, the first vacation, the first "first school day" of the year, the first anniversary, Christmas, birthdays…the list goes on. And it seems endless. All the while, especially during that first year, there is that realization—which still had a newness to it as I awoke almost every morning—that it's all real, that it all happened, and that you're alone. Those first few hundred mornings when the realization that she's gone descends upon you are terrible. And after you get through that first year, you must do it all again.

I know that sounds terrible. But it is. That's the reality of it. And it hurts a lot.

But you also try to make the best of it—especially when you have two little guys in your care who, despite their loss, are looking forward to life and all the things it offers. In fact, if it hadn't been for the two of them, I'm not sure I could have survived—at least survived in relatively good condition physically and emotionally. They were my engine.

I made sure they got to play organized baseball and basketball during these years—things they likely would have done had Carol been with us. I coached Matt's church league basketball team for a year or two, and Pax was old enough to help me run the practices. That provided a strong foundation for our shared love of the game that lasts to this day. Again, families helped enormously with logistics and emotional support. School was OK for them. Like most boys, they didn't particularly like it, but both did well.

More importantly, they seemed well adjusted. Both developed friends and wove themselves nicely into social groups at school and in our neighborhood.

The only problem during this period of any note that I recall was mine. Much as I tried that first year to make things work, I became increasingly depressed. And I mean clinically depressed. In those days, we didn't think in such terms, but I remember my doctor (a good family practitioner) quizzing me about my life and attitude and concluding that I was depressed. I remember telling him I hadn't cried from about the age of five until Carol was diagnosed, but that now, after she was gone, even the simplest things could push me over the edge.

He strongly suggested a small dose of Prozac each day, and I complied. Although it generated some strange dreams at first, once I acclimated to it, I was in better shape. I remember having a visual of being able in my mind to push all—well, maybe not all but some of it—the sadness, loneliness, and everything else into a corner of my brain and closing a door to keep them trapped and away from me. That wasn't happiness by any means. I knew all that was still there. But the medicine took the edge off a bit and gave me some solace and room to work through that first year.

I took myself off Prozac (gradually and under my doctor's supervision) after a year and found I could function reasonably well without it. In fact, after Carol had been gone for three or four years, I remember realizing one day that I was content—not happy but content. After what I'd been through, "content" was quite good enough for me. I had long since given up any hope of real happiness—at least in any romantic sense. But seeing that my boys hadn't crashed and burned after several years, I was pleased and began to think maybe I wouldn't screw it up too badly. Once that "you're gonna screw this up" thing was somewhat behind me (it's never completely gone), I could relax a bit. It took a long time to get to that point—it seemed like forever—but once I got there, I did find some solace or relief.

Don't get me wrong. Like any family, we had our ups and downs. Matt was strong willed (and infuriatingly smart at times), and his will sometimes didn't mix well with my temper. My family knows I came by my temper honestly. My father had a raging one that could spring into action in a split second. Neither my dad nor I were very quiet when we lost our tempers.

I had struggled with mine for years—well before Carol passed and in large measure at her insistence. I don't think I was ever as bad as my dad, but I was hard on the boys at times—particularly Matt, as he began to grow into his teens. We had some loud and assertive arguments, and there were times when I got physical with him.

I suppose a man reflects and softens as he grows older. I know I've regretted some of my words and actions toward both my boys for years now. But I also know that they know I love them and wish I could take some of those things back. To any younger guys who may read this—you can't take it back. All you can do is apologize, but that's never enough. So, the best I can offer is don't even let it become a problem.

I can't let the discussion of Matt's will and my temper pass without recounting the moment I saw the light in his eyes go out. By the lights going out, I mean all respect (indeed it seemed like all regard for me) simply evaporated and was there no longer. We were visiting my eldest sister and her family in Rome, New York. We weren't hockey fans, but my sister and her family were very big on the sport. Matt was twelve, and my nephew was playing high school hockey. During the day, we had a nice breakfast, lunch, and dinner on the way to the hockey game. My sister mentioned—very casually—that we might get some wings after the hockey game. Matt maintains, by the way, that we had no lunch that day. No matter.

Now, my sister was thin and always in good shape, even though she sometimes ate like a horse. Unfortunately, Matt overheard her comment about the wings. I hadn't thought much about it, especially since during the game Matt had eaten a bag of popcorn, I think a hotdog, and some candy. So, as the hockey game ended, we got up to leave. Instead of walking toward the aisle up the bleachers, Matt turned full face to me and asked, "What are we going to do now?"

"I guess we're going to (my sister)'s," I said.

"No. Really?" he said, as if he thought I was kidding.

I was perplexed and said, "Yes. Really."

Matt's response was to look at me with absolute disdain and to repeat several times in a very loud voice, "What? Man! Really? Aw, man. Gosh, man." And he kept repeating these words loudly. The tone of disgust and the decibel level of his voice made it clear to everyone within earshot that I was being dressed down by this snarky twelve-year-old boy. No father wants to be spoken to like that by anyone, much less his son. But what bothered me the most was that just before he broke into his deriding mantra directed at me, I literally saw the light in his eyes dim. Maybe it was an optical illusion, but I think I saw the lights go down, if not out completely. At the very least, I'm sure this was the moment when he descended into teenage-hood—that period of life during which the man he once revered as capable of almost anything has suddenly become one of the dumbest asses to ever walk the earth.

As it turned out, Matt's "seizure" was to last approximately ten years. And it dissipated only gradually. It was during that period that I handled myself and my temper poorly at times. But I'll always remember when his vacation from rationality began—a high school hockey game in Rome, New York. All in all, I still think that's a funny story to which virtually every man raising a son can relate to.

It was during this first few years that the boys and I established the three major pillars of our lives together—basketball, music, and humor. These clearly weren't the sole bases of the relationships among the three of us, but they did provide a continuing and abiding source of mutual enjoyment—primarily enjoyment of one another. We still circle around these things. I'm sure most families have similar centers of focus, but these were ours and they continue to serve each of us well.

I mentioned our love of basketball earlier. This was the first pillar. During these first few years, in addition to the boys playing in organized leagues, we all enjoyed going out to a court ourselves and playing around. I was always somewhat of a coach to them in many things, but especially when it came to basketball.

Instead of merely shooting around, we began to play games. At six and seven years of age, Pax found it difficult to compete. And Matt wasn't all that much of a challenge to me in those days at eleven or twelve. So, we simply changed the rules. Pax got a point if he hit the net, two if he hit the rim, and four or five if he made a shot. Of course, we were lax in enforcing other rules like walking, double dribbles, and the like. Matt's rules were somewhat more stringent than Pax's, but still loose enough to accommodate his lack of size and skills.

We also adjusted the rules so that each of us was a team of one. It was always the guy with the ball going against two defensive guys. It sounds unfair, but we made it work. For example, if a defensive guy blocked a shot out of bounds, he got the ball because of his good defensive play. If it went out of bounds without a block, he could still get the ball if the shooter attributed his miss to good defense.

I know it sounds simplistic, but it was complicated as those rules developed over time. More importantly, the success of those rules depended on honesty and personal integrity. You called your own fouls. You gave the other guy credit for good defense. The list goes on. We came to respect each other as well as the game.

I was never one of those dads who let their kids win every game. I wanted them to understand that, even at a young age, excessive traveling or other offenses had consequences. I always tried to make sure the games were competitive so that, at the end, anyone had a chance to win.

We also enjoyed watching basketball together. As any coaching dad knows, TV sports is often an excellent opportunity to teach kids about a game by showing how the good pros do it. Plus, and I will admit I influenced my sons greatly in this, we were all Boston Celtics fans. I'd watched the Celtics from the late fifties all through the sixties and seventies, and it wasn't hard to convert Matt and Pax into true Celtics believers. The fun we had (and the pain we experienced) watching them play still echoes in our brains.

More on basketball later. For now, suffice it to say that it has been, and continues to be, one of the most important things around which we three have related to one another. Basketball has always provided us with a common and abiding interest—a sport to play, to watch, to discuss, and to argue about (good-naturedly, of course).

A second pillar of our relationship has been music. From the days when they were but a year old, especially on Friday evenings when the pressures of work were put out of mind, Carol and I would gather in the living room to play music—usually the Beatles in those days—and maybe have a glass of wine. I know that "Beatles" will sound trite to some. But unless you were there—that is, aware of music in the sixties—it's difficult to understand what those guys did, how well they did it, and the sea change they brought about in music.

Even before he reached twelve months of age, Matt would sit in my lap as I sat cross-legged on the living-room floor, and I would move his arms to the cadence of the music. Over his first few years, I taught him to listen first to percussion—only percussion. Then to the bass and the bass only. Then to rhythm guitar, then lead, and so on. He learned a lot about how songs were constructed and intuitively how each part could relate to other parts so inventively. He saw the magic of music (rock music at least) early on and continues to enjoy it today, as we all do.

By the time Pax came along and was old enough to sit in my lap, Matt would listen for a while. But at eight o'clock, he would abandon his family to watch his favorite TV series—*The Dukes of Hazzard*. God help me, *The Dukes of Hazzard*! I hated that, but what are you gonna say to a four-year-old whose buddies expected him to know what had happened on the Friday-night episode.

Back to music. Pax went through the same process Matt did, learning to break the music down to better understand how well its parts comprised a whole song.

We did listen to a lot of music aside from the Beatles—much more. And, as the boys grew older, each was to discover more and bring it to the other two of us.

After Carol passed, music continued to play an important role in our lives together. We would play it at least 70 percent of the time we were in a car—especially if the drive was more than a few minutes. In fact, it was not unusual for me to take several detours on the way home if an album was not quite finished just so we could see (or hear) it to the end. I'm sure I must have spent several hundred dollars in gas over the years just for the sake of listening to music we love.

A shared sense of humor was the third pillar we rallied around. I suppose every dad feels like it's his job in some respects to make things good for his kids. And part of that is making them laugh. I had always been good at that, but after our loss—especially the first few years—it was hard work. I just didn't feel like it most of the time. But you try—you try because you know it's what the boys need—and because, hard as it might be—you need it too.

Then, over time, a funny thing begins to happen—you notice, little by little, that you're getting some satisfaction (not quite pleasure—that was still unattainable in my mind) out of making them laugh. I knew they still hurt and missed their mom. But when they laughed, it was like I could remove those things for at least a few seconds. Like I say, satisfaction, if not pleasure. And for me to hear them laugh was (or at least became over time) music. It's gonna sound corny as heck, but the fact is I can still hear each of their laughs in my head. I can see the smiles and looks in their eyes. Each memory of the boys' laughter and expressions is distinctive from the others. Like I said, they were my engine. Neat.

The result of my many attempts to bring them to laughter was a long series of long-standing "inside jokes" among the three of us. Just stupid things that guys laugh about. We still laugh about them today—or at least remember them fondly. We all remember the songs I used to sing to them constructed from popular melodies but with my own lyrics. Songs like "I Want to be Rich" sung to the melody of "I've Got to Be Me." Or my own version of "I'm an Old Cowhand."

I tried to soften the humor in those early months when I noticed our increasing hardness, and to some extent, I think I succeeded. As the boys grew older, though, that became somewhat more difficult. Guys are just harder on each other as a rule than girls. But in the end, I think it turned out OK. Both have a well-developed sense of humor, and neither is terribly rough on anyone, including their own kids.

## Looking Back

Except for our humor, basketball games, music, and Matt's descent into teenage-hood, I honestly don't have too many specific recollections of events during these first few years after Carol's death—at least not many that serve a purpose here except to illustrate further the fear, the hurt, and all those things I tried to describe and illustrate earlier.

I know I worried about Pax because he was so young (and seemingly vulnerable) back then. I think he might have been most affected by the loss of Carol in terms of finding his role among us and maybe with other kids too. He was only five, and all his friends and classmates had moms. I think he just needed to figure things out for himself, but I wish I'd been of more help to him. But as he grew, it became clear he was gonna be just fine. In fact, in many ways he's turned out to be more socially adept than Matt or me. The point is, though, that had Carol been around, I don't think he'd have felt so out of place at times during those early years.

I find it curious that my recollection of specific things during these first few years is so lacking. I think it's because it was during this time that I was most worried about how we would fare and was just trying to get through each day. I remember thinking what drudgery it was except when I was with the boys.

As the years passed, both boys have mentioned to me or their wives how happy and neat their childhoods were. They sometimes speak of things I'd long since forgotten and which I would never have thought could mean much to them. But they apparently did. Like any parent, I take a certain amount of pride in that—and more than a little satisfaction.

Truth is, I think the games we invented, the music we played, and the humor we shared were the first signs of our collective healing. Eventually, they became a large part of the foundation of our next twenty years together. Back then, I don't think I fully appreciated the importance of those games, the music, and the humor. I do now. Though they are now forty and thirty-five years of age, I still remember the looks on their faces and the sounds of their laughter so long ago when we succeeded in amusing one another.

Basketball and music will get more attention as I address later years here. Suffice it to say here that those things and our shared sense of humor will always be important to us, if for no other reason than that they provided something around which we rallied and shared when we needed them most.

# 12
# Getting On With It

After the first two or three years, we settled into a routine of sorts. My work certainly kept me busy, and it was during this period that both our families stepped forward to help with the boys while I did my job and tended to my career. My work was probably not much more demanding than other lawyers experienced, but my company was going through some difficult times, and because of the area of experience and knowledge I had accumulated during the previous ten years, I was best placed to deal with much of what was troubling the company. And to do so required a fair amount of travel, primarily between Charleston, West Virginia, where we were raising the boys, and Houston, Texas. In fact, from 1988 (three years after Carol died) until mid-1991, the company maintained an apartment for my use in Houston.

Being away so much was hard. Much as I enjoyed my work, I missed the boys and often felt guilty that I wasn't around more than I was. Recall that we are all basketball guys—we love the sport and are fans to this day. I coached the boys' church-league basketball teams in the first few years after losing Carol. Although I coached Pax's teams through his sixth-grade year, my attendance at practice was spottier than I would have liked. But after that year, I didn't do much coaching of their teams and seemed to be gone more and more often.

Matt was in his teens by then, and I was missing a lot of his high-school basketball games. I did my best to be there when I could, but sometimes it just wasn't possible. I remember several times driving straight from the airport to some outlying rural school to see at least part of his games. But I never was there enough for my satisfaction, and I know Matt felt my absence and mentioned it a few times. I felt particularly bad for him because he wanted so badly to play ball and play well. And he did just that. His problem was that he simply wasn't blessed with the kind of physical equipment his brother and I were. He's not quite six feet tall—he developed asthma at an early age and was just never fast with his feet. He was a smart basketball player and hustled a lot. But he knew high school was his limit, and so did I. Wish I could have made more of his games. I have always thought that of the guys I played ball with (including most in college), he got the most out of what he had. And I played ball with a lot of guys, a few of whom played in the NBA.

I was able to be a bit more consistent attending practices and games with Pax's teams as I coached them. In fact, when he was in the first grade, our church couldn't find enough kids to play in the third and fourth grade league. Nor could they find a coach. I volunteered to coach if the league would let first and second graders play.

They agreed, so I coached a team that lost every game that season by huge margins. Scores in the range of 26–4 were not uncommon. Obviously, we weren't terribly talented, but we did have a pretty good third grader, Pax, and another first grader named Clint. They did their best but simply weren't very good that first year. The second year was better. I'm not sure whether we won any games or not, but they were reasonably competitive. I remember those first two years; the parents of kids from opposing teams would cheer our boys whenever they scored.

By the time Pax got into the third grade, he, Clint, and the kid one year ahead of them knew what they were doing. They tore through the league that year. Then in the fifth and sixth grade league, they won as well. By the time Pax ended his sixth grade season, those opposing teams' parents were booing us most of the time. It was kind of sad to hear, but we lived through it. It was a lot of fun developing those guys into a cohesive group that worked so well together. Pax obviously enjoyed it, and Matt was into it as well. He loved watching his younger brother play. All in all, those four years brought us closer together. More importantly, those years served to provide Pax with the knowledge that he could find his role and achieve things. He knew his coach depended on him heavily to do his job and help his teammates do theirs. It was so neat to be able to see him develop so up close and personal.

As a teenager, Matt was in some ways very typical. He often couldn't (or didn't want to) see why things sometimes didn't work out his way. And when they didn't, he could be vocal about it. In other ways, he was anything but typical. Some of the things he did—just because they needed doing—were remarkable. Remarkable not just because he didn't need to be told or asked to do them, but because he just did them. And some of those things were adult things—often for his brother's benefit. After Matt began to drive, for example, he would make sure Pax was where he needed to be to meet his commitments. He would often help the series of housekeepers I brought in to stay with them when I was out of town (family couldn't be there all the time) by telling them how we preferred things done in the house.

Perhaps the best example of Matt's maturity occurred about three months after his sixteenth birthday and his acquisition of his first driver's license. For two or three years, we'd had various women outside of family come into the house when I was gone to perform basic housecleaning chores, be there when the boys got home from school, and to stay overnight just to have an adult around.

Matt came to me and told me that while these ladies were all very nice, it never felt to the boys like they had their home to themselves with a stranger staying with them. He pointed out that both my mom and his aunt (Carol's sister) lived within about a mile from our home and that Carol's parents were only twenty to thirty minutes away by car. He assured me that if I left enough cash and a reasonably stocked kitchen, he could and would make sure that both he and Pax were fed well and that they would both be where they needed to be to meet their school and social commitments. Finally, he assured me that upon my return, he would provide receipts and cash that when added together would equal the cash I'd left in his care.

It's worth noting that most of my trips during this period were multinight trips. It wasn't unusual for me to be gone for three or four nights in a row. I thought about his proposal for a few days and consulted all three of his living grandparents. No one thought it was too much for Matt to handle. Of course, I extracted the usual promises from him that there would be no visitors or parties in our home with me out of town—there would be no going out with friends even if Pax were to go along. And relatives from both sides of the family stood ready to help if needed.

So, I gave it a try. A short trip first, followed by longer ones until Matt's proposal became the norm. Yeah, I worried a little at first. But I'd always told Carol (and anyone else who would listen) that Matt was born "going on forty-five years of age." He just always seemed to act older than his years. But after a couple of months, I never gave it much thought. It seemed and felt right and met just about every criterion I'd set for him over the course of the next couple of years.

That whole experiment started in July 1991. I know I estimated the amount of money I'd have paid women to come babysit over the next six months, but I can't remember what the estimate was. What I do remember is getting Matt alone sometime that next December, telling him how friggin' proud I was of what he'd done, and giving him a check for a thousand dollars. It might have been two thousand, but I'm not sure. Even a thousand dollars in 1991 for a sixteen-year-old boy was a pretty good sum of money. I told him the check wasn't a Christmas gift—it was something I felt he'd earned and deserved. I've never thought otherwise.

As a young boy, Pax was somewhat less assertive by nature

than me or his brother. The basketball experience from the first through the sixth grades was very good for him, but that didn't change his nature fundamentally. As he got into his teens, it became clear to me that what I took as a lesser level of assertiveness was simply a longer fuse than either Matt or I had.

There was no mistaking his assertiveness on a basketball court. In fact, some of the things he did while playing ball were remarkable. I had a decent high-school career and rode a scholarship to a Division One school when I was young. I don't claim to be anything extraordinary as a basketball analyst, but it's not rocket science, and I'm no slouch when it comes to evaluating talent.

Between the ages of nine or ten and fourteen, Pax did things on a basketball court that simply can't be taught. His nose for the ball and feel for the game were developed beyond his years. His passing game was creative. Anyone from almost any sport will tell you that "reading" a situation involving multiple players and then manipulating them to open a passing lane is special in a young kid. Pax had real talent.

And he was naturally good at things that could be taught. Like his dad, his ball handling could have been a bit better, but his jump shot was smooth and consistent. I'm not saying he was good enough to play in the NBA, but he was good for his age back then. I watched him in one game at about age eleven, with a combination of steals and shots, score eight points in five seconds. Impressive.

I think what I'm trying to say is that I was unfair to Pax for a long time in the way I thought of him off the court. I tended to view him in slightly the same way my mother did—more vulnerable than he was because he'd lost his mom at the tender age of five. After her death, he's the one I worried about the most just because of his young age. I knew (or thought) he was gonna miss his mom's influence in ways he might not recognize until he became an adult. I didn't carry that view to any extreme but I was bad enough.

My mom, on the other hand, carried that feeling to extremes. She seemed to always treat Pax as if he were about two to four years younger than he was. She even bought Pax a present one year on Matt's birthday because she didn't want him to feel bad or left out.

Though I wasn't as bad about that as Mom, my overblown sense of his vulnerability had consequences. One was that, too often, I underestimated him.

Matt was the first to bring all this to my attention in explicit terms. They are about four and a half years apart in age and for significant parts of their childhoods attended the same schools. Matt (never shy with his opinion, as I've said before) told me as early as Pax's seventh or eighth grade year that Pax was well liked and considered by his peers as one of the "go to" guys—one of the classmates whose thoughts about various things were important to others. They may or may not have always sought them out, but they did watch his reactions to various events and circumstances. Even Matt's friends, despite the four-plus years' difference in age, seemed to enjoy having Pax around as one of their crowd. I suspect Pax's prowess on the basketball court helped too.

I understood what Matt was saying and accepted it. But it's hard to fully internalize such things unless and until one sees it in action. I wish I'd had a better appreciation of Matt's point in those days, but I was so busy with work and trying to keep everything else together I didn't have enough time to just observe him and his interactions with other kids in depth. At least that's what I tell myself now. Carol would not have let that happen.

This period of life without Carol was when our humor began to flourish. True to every father's aspiration to make his kids laugh, and perhaps feeling a bit freer about what I could joke about without a lady around, I did my best to create incidents of humor for all of us to enjoy. If I noticed a particularly large number of Taco Bells on a short stretch of interstate, I would accuse them of traveling in herds. If we needed a butter substitute (it was the nineties, and we didn't know these substitutes weren't so good for you), I would send Matt into the store, intentionally forgetting the name of the product and substituting my own name for it, like "Don't tell me that s—t's not butter."

I recognize most of the humor was juvenile. But that's what these boys were back then—juvenile. We had dozens of these and other running jokes, all of which provided us some amusement and many of which illustrated for the boys how language can be used inventively to entertain.

And we each brought humor to our time together. In fact, this is another area where Pax's cleverness and intellect began to shine through. His wit diffused more than a few situations between Matt and me. And he was downright funny for no particular reason at times.

We took an extended vacation during this period—my first since joining my company some nine or ten years before. We spent three weeks driving west, first to Colorado Springs where we spent three or four days sight-seeing, relaxing and just doing whatever we wanted to do. Unfortunately, Matt and I engaged in some real donnybrooks during this trip. Ever expressive about his opinions on what we should do and when we should do it, Matt rarely held back.

I don't think I would have minded his opinion quite so much if it hadn't been accompanied with the "attitude." He tended to express his thoughts in the same way he dressed me down at the hockey game in Rome, New York, some years before. That is to say, he clearly believed I was pretty much a dumb ass, and that came through loud and clear. I'll not lie. It pissed me off more than a couple of times. And we Jarrell males don't handle "pissed off" very well. I know I didn't. Too often, my reaction as the adult was not very adult-like. I reverted too often to what I'd seen from my dad as a boy: very high anger with loud cussing and sometimes physical action. Not good.

Matt sometimes didn't handle things too well either. But I

was the adult—or should have been. But even knowing then he might have done better, I always admired his refusal to back down, even in the face of a very angry father who was bigger than him.

To this day, losing my temper with Matt—and sometimes, but not nearly as often with Pax—is one of my greatest regrets. No excuses—no rationalizing. Just a big mistake repeated too many times. Parents should take note that such exchanges with your children may not be that meaningful taken individually. But when they become routine (or even semi routine), they can be harmful. And it's the adult's job to find ways to end that cycle. I wish I'd been better at that.

We swung down from Colorado to the Four Corners area and then back home via the southern route (New Mexico, Texas, Arkansas, Tennessee, Kentucky, and then to West Virginia). In spite of Matt's and my blowups, we all had a great time. We stopped at many places and saw many sights along the way—Carlsbad Caverns, Six Flags Park near Dallas, my sister and her family in East Texas, and Mammoth Caves in Kentucky. I loved those weeks with them, especially after all the time I'd spent away from home.

This period also saw the continued development of our special form of basketball. As I've explained, the rules were always subject to revision as the boys matured and became more capable and competitive. As they both entered their teens, the rules changed dramatically. I was getting older, and they were both getting stronger. And the games became more intense. We were a competitive trio, and these games only served to feed our need to compete. We had succeeded in making the rules of the game we played quite equal so that, on any given day, anyone had a shot at winning any game—and I was no longer engineering the closeness of those games. There were times when we would find a gym and play for three or four hours at a time. I was in my forties and not wholly incapable, but this kind of intensity was meant for younger guys.

Most importantly, though, we had fun. Yeah, with three competitive guys, there are going to be some dustups—arguments about certain things. But as a rule, we avoided anything serious. Damn, those were fun times.

Our mutual admiration and enjoyment of music also became deeper. Those detours to finish off an album or a song were more frequent. As Pax put it once, it was almost like a religion. And Matt especially, was intent on learning to play the guitar. He read magazines and taught himself many of the technical aspects of music I knew little about.

Pax too made his foray into playing instruments—bass and keyboards. He joined a band in high school and played at a few venues. I don't think I was invited, but he and his band played several times at a coffee shop downtown. Wish I could have seen it. I'm sure it wasn't all that smooth, but I loved that these boys and their friends would give things like that a try. For the most part, I would have been much too shy and insecure to do such a thing.

I was not a father who spoiled his sons, but there were two instances during the year I would splurge on. First was vacation. They were so important to me, and we each loved the beach so much, I didn't mind spending a bit extra so we could rent houses on the beach each year. The boys seemed to enjoy those times as well. Pax, true to his "gift" with the ladies (I still don't get it, but you'll see what I mean in the next section) even had a romance or two during these trips.

The second splurge was Christmas. I wasn't given to buying a lot of toys that would be forgotten after six months and end up in the basement. But if my sons wanted instruments or amplifiers or microphones or other equipment so they could enjoy their music and maybe even develop whatever talent they might have, I was willing to provide those things. They knew I would, but neither ever seemed to abuse that knowledge by asking for too much. And I always enjoyed seeing that equipment being used as it was intended to be used. They both put that stuff to good use.

One more thing about this period—and I'm speaking generally about two years after Carol's death through about six years after. I didn't date. I still had that inescapable feeling that everything romantic in my life was in the rearview mirror. I had put my head down and was concentrating on work and the boys. I felt quite strongly that I could never again feel for anyone else what I'd felt for Carol. Probably not the healthiest outlook on life to have, but this was to change with time.

I did begin seeing a very nice lady in Houston toward the end of this period, but I wouldn't call it dating. Although there was affection between us, we both knew nothing serious would ever develop. I was too wrapped up raising the boys, and she had her own life events to deal with. She was a nice and attractive lady who needed an escort from time to time to bank functions (her employer). And I sometimes needed a date for the same sort of thing. It was a nice friendship that never turned physical. But as my work took me away from Houston more and more in 1991, we drifted apart and lost contact.

I never told the boys about her until years later. I wasn't embarrassed by it, but knowing it wasn't going to go anywhere, I just didn't think telling them would serve any purpose. Since they were relatively young, I didn't think it was a great idea for them to be exposed to a relationship that, good as it was, was merely a matter of convenience.

## Looking Back

It's a little hard looking back at this period just as it was for the first two years, and I'm not quite sure why. It's probably due to a continuation of my being so busy with both work and the boys that it's all just a blur to me now. I do remember, though, that our ability to tease one another and find things to laugh about taught me in a rudimentary way that if you smile—even when you don't feel like it—it can improve your outlook.

And with some persistence, you begin to smile too and to mean it.

Then there was our music and basketball. Fun activities to be sure, but the more I think about it, their importance was in providing quality time with my sons. Again, not specific memories of many events of great significance—just the general recollection that our time spent engaged in those pursuits was healing too and healthy for us in a variety of ways. I do remember that our music was the focus of many discussions about why this was good and that wasn't so good. And those discussions were surprisingly sophisticated.

Because of humor, music, and basketball playing such a huge factor in our lives, that feeling of utter sadness and hopelessness gradually—and over a pretty extended period—morphed into something resembling contentment. Not happiness, mind you, but contentment. After so many years of sadness and fear, I was just so glad to be at that point. Not that I had dwelled on things too much, but I don't think I had hope for happiness. Even knowing that Carol would not have wanted me to stop living and not be sad didn't help. It just made me miss her more.

As this realization that I was content dawned on me, I did everything I could to embrace it. I remember being so pleased. Not excited but pleased. I remember thinking, "OK, if this is as good as it's going to get, I can live with this." At least I felt— or was beginning to feel—that I had a life again. And from where I'd started, that was quite remarkable.

# 13

# The Hard Part of Raising Kids
# (1991–1997)

Kids are hard to raise—no secret there. But there is great joy and satisfaction too. The sad part is that much of that joy and satisfaction isn't realized until they're gone and out of the house. True, you can and do enjoy the process while they're with you. But you also deal with all the issues that arise—their "growing up" issues, the issues that arise simply because people have lived together for ten to twenty years. After they leave, though, those distractions tend to fade into the background.

By 1991–1992, the boys and I had reached some sort of equilibrium—a comfortable pattern. Pax was still playing basketball, though my coaching days were just about over. Matt had settled into his teens and, except for a somewhat irritating insistence that things should go his way at times (in the past, I would have said all the time), was a solid and responsible kid. He was always there to make sure Pax was OK when I had to travel—which was often in those days—and he seemed to do well in school. He was every bit the kid I identified when he was three or four years of age as "born going on forty-five."

Our humor continued as a constant in our lives. And I guess I saw my role (especially as the boys grew older) as the guy who would "push the envelope" to get a laugh. One such occasion occurred during a trip to Wrightsville Beach in North Carolina. As we arrived on our first Saturday afternoon, the clouds opened up, and it rained hard with some lightening for a few hours after we checked in—not good weather for spending time in the ocean. So, we played a couple of games of Monopoly. When the sun finally broke through, we hit the deck of the duplex I had rented with a nice view of the ocean and the street just beside our duplex, which provided access to the beach and various shops a block or so inland.

OK, I'd had a beer or two. So, when the boys spied two young girls in bikinis (maybe fifteen or sixteen years old) walking on the street, they did what any boys would do. They discretely moved closer to the edge of the deck for a better look. Any father stands ready to take advantage of almost any chance to embarrass his kids. Outta nowhere and far enough back from the edge of the deck to avoid detection by the young girls, using my best "drunken voice"—think Barney from the Simpsons—I yelled, "Hello. We're up here. We…we have beer!"

The girls, of course, turned to see who was speaking to them and immediately focused on the boys before they could retreat to where they couldn't be seen. Of course, both boys were embarrassed and pretty critical of what I thought was a funny event. They admonished me long and severely for what they saw as an unwarranted and kinda cheap trick. The admonitions fell on deaf ears, though, in large part because they were delivered by two guys who knew what I'd done was funny and couldn't help but laugh.

To this day, when one of the three of us sees a pretty girl, there is usually a "We have beer" shout-out just to let the others know to look. Most often the shout isn't loud enough to be heard by the pretty girl. And in spite of their repetition, those words never fail to amuse us. My daughters-in-law may differ with my assessment of "amused," but so be it.

The only problems Matt presented beyond the occasional snarky behavior were minor. Perhaps that's best exemplified by the time I awoke on a weekend and found scratches mixed with red paint on the passenger side of my car. Matt had been to a party the evening before. Like most parents upon discovering prominent scratches along the side of my car, I wondered if he had scraped up against something while driving and drinking. I had him come and look at the scratches. Of course, he immediately proclaimed his ignorance and declared that one of the other kids must have sideswiped him while entering or leaving the yard the kids had parked in. I thought something was amiss both because Matt couldn't recall any of his buddies driving a red car and because…well, just because. There was something in the way he talked about it that led me to believe he knew more than he was saying.

He also assured me he hadn't been drinking. Now, I didn't buy Matt's full story that morning. But I did believe him when he told me he hadn't been drinking. He's never shown much, if any, interest in alcohol, and I trusted him on that issue.

I did dress him down slightly for the damage and let him know it couldn't happen again. But frankly, at age sixteen or seventeen, when a kid has been at the root of so few problems, and the damage is a few scratches, I wasn't inclined to make a big deal about it. It's worth noting (from my point of view anyway) that, to this day and usually when I'm challenging the veracity of something he's said, Matt will still say something like "I swear, Dad. It was another car with red paint." Uh-huh.

Pax was doing well during this period too. His basketball skills had matured with age, and he was clearly among the better players in his age group at age twelve through fifteen or sixteen. It was during the latter part of this period when Pax began to become the darling of his female classmates in school. At about the eighth or ninth grade, a good athlete with reasonable looks was going to get some attention from girls. But the level of attention Pax got was high—silly, really.

What irritated his brother and me the most was the attention from the mothers of his classmates. After games, many of these grown women made over Pax like he was some sort of teddy bear. Some of the thirty- and forty-year-old women would literally fawn over him—not quite flirting but almost. So, we'll call it "fawning." Neither Matt nor I could understand why these females showed him so much attention while ignoring the two of us. Some of these women were single, and by then, I was just about ready to entertain the idea of another relationship.

I don't think Pax ever realized fully how much attention he got from girls and grown women—at least not until after he married the woman who became my younger daughter-in-law. When Pax was in his twenties, he and I walked through a bar one evening to join his wife. While I was following Pax, I noticed several glances from very attractive girls and at least one pretty overt flirt. He was in his mid- to late twenties by then.

I mentioned the flirt to my daughter-in-law, intending to tease or embarrass Pax. It didn't work. Her response was to wave her hand and politely tell me that it happened all the time. She was not bothered by it in the least. Ya gotta love the confidence.

But it bothered me. Everywhere we went for years— especially after Pax got to his middle teens—people remarked at how much Pax resembled me. If that was so, why is it I never got that kind of attention? Just didn't, and doesn't, seem fair.

It was at about this time that I lost Matt in a sense. I'd never thought his departure from home for college was going to affect me much at all. Frankly, I didn't give it much thought. The empty-nest syndrome was something that affected mothers, primarily at least. Not dads like me. Live and learn.

I had bought Matt a small used car, and he had decided on a small liberal-arts school about four and a half hours from our home. Our plan was to leave Pax with Carol's folks, pack both Matt's car and mine, and move him down to his new school. On our way out of town, we were going to pick up a guitar Matt had decided to buy (he'd been shopping for some weeks) from a place near the entrance to the interstate we were to take to his school. We got the guitar, loaded it in his car, and took off.

But eighteen-year-olds are still teenagers. And while Matt

was a bright kid, he occasionally did eighteen-year-old stuff. Instead of going east on the interstate, he went west. Not a horrible mistake in and of itself. But he was moving and left me in the dust. I had no idea where he'd gone, and as hard as I tried, I had no luck in finding him on the interstate.

Now, cell phones were not universally available in those days, so there was no way I could contact him quickly. I drove west. I turned around and came back east—always trying to figure out what he would have done and where he might have gone. After about thirty minutes of searching, I called home, hoping to leave a message for him that he would get. I told him where to meet me—about 120 miles from our hometown.

I kept driving east toward his school, all the while searching for him ahead or behind me, or headed in the opposite direction on the other side of the interstate median. There was a time when I thought I saw a hand waving outside a silver-blue car (the color of his car) in the westbound lanes but quickly dismissed it as being a real possibility. But as I drove, I thought if that was him waving at me, surely he would turn around and head east. So, I pulled to the side of the interstate and waited.

After twenty minutes or so, dusk was approaching. It had been a good hour and a half since he'd gone off course, and I was getting a little worried. Before I knew it, a state trooper pulled up behind me as I stood beside my car. This trooper wasn't much older than Matt. He asked me what I was doing. I explained that I'd lost my college-age son. He laughed but told me I'd have to move along. I did.

I went to the place where I told Matt I'd meet him. No Matt there. After dark, I went a bit farther down the road and checked into a motel. Now, throughout my travels that day, I kept calling home, hoping he would have the same idea as I did and leave a message for me. Nothing.

After I got to my room, I began calling grandparents, aunts, and anyone else I could think of, asking if they'd heard from my wayward child. No one had. Even the next morning, no one had heard from this boy. I drove on down to his school, where registration was in progress. I found his academic advisor and learned that Matt had yet to appear.

Worried to death, I strolled out into the late-August sunshine just in time to see the small blue-silver car tooling into town and looking for a place to park. Jeez, the relief. Maybe I shouldn't have been, but I was worried about him. Not knowing where he was or what had happened scared the bejesus out of me.

My relief was short-lived. When he saw me, Matt whipped his car around a corner, turned to me and with a stern look on his face, pointed his finger at me and jerked it to the passenger seat, telling me—by his gestures alone—in no uncertain terms to get my ass over there, now. Remarkable how quickly relief can turn to anger when confronted with attitude.

I forget exactly what was said in those first few minutes, but neither of us was happy with the other. Thing is, I had no idea what I'd done wrong to merit this fit of snarkiness from my eldest son. I still have no idea. The only thing I could ever deduce is that he maybe thought the best defense was a good offense.

I have had much enjoyment over the years telling this story in much greater detail than I have here. And that detail has been at Matt's expense. He remains convinced that I have embellished his error unfairly, and he might be right. But I don't think so.

What I do know is that (1) he made a boneheaded wrong turn, (2) he quickly turned around and drove about thirty miles east from our hometown, whereupon (3) he realized he'd forgotten to pack a tie, which was required for registration at this rather preppy school, so (4) he drove thirty miles west all the way home to retrieve a tie—never thinking he might avoid a sixty-mile round trip by simply buying a tie on the way to school.

Oh. And the hand from the silver-blue car headed west? That was him.

We discussed the matter for a while before we got him registered. We both had our say. I took him to dinner and left. Then it hit. This kid with whom I and his brother had been through so much had left home, and it was never gonna be the same.

I observed earlier in these pages how I never cried between the ages of five and thirty-one, when Carol was diagnosed. Well, I made up for quite a bit of that on the drive home. Not fun. I missed him immediately.

The biggest thing for Pax during this period was what I saw as a periodic lack of certainty—a self-consciousness—which I thought was not warranted. I'm not sure if "uncertainty" is the right word here, but it's the best I can think of. As I've mentioned, Pax was always much more like his mom than me. She wasn't uncertain, but she wasn't assertive until she needed to be. I, on the other hand, am more likely to react assertively in situations much sooner than either of them—sometimes, too soon, I'll admit.

In Pax's case, he didn't seem to be as sure of himself as I and others thought he should be. It was a little different than Carol, but his reticence reminded me a bit of her tendency to be somewhat passive at times. He could be assertive when he needed to be. But as a kid, he had to be pushed far before it kicked in.

I surmised (and to some extent still believe—though I'm no psychologist) that much of what he relied on in his early life was dramatically upended. He saw his mom sick, both of us struggling with the illness, and then his dad reduced to tears and sadness for a year or two. That's probably enough to shake up anyone of any age. But I think it got to him in a way that made him question his instincts sometimes, and maybe because of that his intelligence. I knew the kid was smart and talented, but it sometimes seemed like there was no convincing him of that. So, I figured he just needed to get a little "ballsier" and maybe work a little harder to appreciate where he stood with his peers.

Oddly, I now attribute this lack of sureness in Pax largely to what I now see as a pretty unique take on things. As he progressed through his teen years and grew into adulthood, I was increasingly impressed with how he could look at the same facts as Matt or me or others and come to conclusions or solutions that we—or I, at least—would never have thought of. Interesting. But disappointing that I didn't figure that out earlier. It would have made his teenage years easier for him. At least I think so.

I suppose all parents look back at some things they wish they'd done better. Helping Pax deal more quickly and effectively with this issue is one of those things for me. I was simply slow to recognize that there was an issue and that he was dealing with something I didn't understand. Instead, I assumed Pax just needed a few boots in the backside, and being the typical Jarrell male, I was perfectly willing to deliver them (figuratively, of course).

Even with all that going on, Pax had some stellar moments. He was fifteen or sixteen, and I was coaching his AAU summer basketball team. A high-school gym on a hot, sunny July afternoon with eight or ten guys playing ball can get quite toasty. After the bulk of the practice was over, we began scrimmaging. My assistant coach and I were playing too, because we didn't have many kids that day. We both needed the workout anyway.

I was in my midforties but was in decent shape, always had a shot, and was very experienced on a basketball court. I could control these kids and had proved it several times that summer. At least until this day. Suddenly, outta nowhere, Pax took over. His quickness, decisiveness, inventiveness, and power all combined, and he took over the scrimmage. I'd never (or rarely) associated power with Pax's game. But it was there that day in spades. He took control of that game from me both on defense and offense. It was the only time I thought one of my sons could have been better at the sport than me. God knows they both tried.

At the break, he was vibrating. He knew something had shifted, and he knew what he was doing. I asked him what the hell was going on, and he couldn't explain it. All in all, he handled it all very well.

One more event of significance during this period. I had my first long-term girlfriend whom I introduced to the boys. She flirted with me at a company picnic, and I fell—hard. By this time, I was in my midforties (forty-six, to be exact) and had been alone for well over ten years. And out of the blue, this attractive girl flirts with me.

It had been a long time. Hell, I hadn't even dated in high school and college. And during a very short period when I wasn't dating Carol, I didn't have to work for dates. Consequently, I never (and still don't) considered myself good with women. But I guess I was at least adequate to the task in this case. It was September 13 when she first flirted with me. By the week before Thanksgiving in November, I'd lost close to forty pounds and was running between thirty and thirty-five miles a week.

I dated her for about two and a half years—actually, probably a year and a half longer than I should have. She was a very nice person, but it was clear to me (way down deep) that we weren't meant to be together long term. I'll never be sorry for the time we spent together. It provided me with a whole new perspective on and about life. I wish I'd been fairer to her.

In any event, this relationship was to have a pretty profound impact on me—mostly favorable. For the first time since losing Carol, I realized I could love someone without feeling guilty—without comparing what I was feeling with how I felt about Carol. Maybe even more importantly, I felt worthy of being loved. It might sound odd, but when you think all the romance in your life is over for so long a period of time, you begin to wonder whether anyone could love you. Eventually, that wondering skews toward conviction. It's an insidious and destructive thing. Not healthy. So that explains why I lost so much weight in such a short period.

On the other hand, I must confess that this episode distracted me for the first time from my primary job—raising my sons. Indeed, for about a year, I failed to spend as much time with Pax as I should have. In fact, there were far too many unsupervised evenings and nights. He handled it reasonably well, but he was only about sixteen and needed me more than I realized. He didn't get into serious trouble during that period, but he was left to drift on his own too many evenings. I'm sure the timing of my distraction didn't help with his issues. Again, I felt like I let him down. Only it was my fault, and I had everything to do with it. Regrets. We all have them, I suppose. This one has been unpleasant to live with.[3]

This period also saw the most intensity in our basketball together. I was now in my mid to late forties, Matt was in his late teens and early twenties, and Pax was coming into his own physically. Jeez, we played hard. But again, there were only a few arguments about the games. The one exception was Matt blaming me for an ankle injury when he came down on my foot. He ended up wearing a boot for a few weeks and claimed I'd been unduly careless in trying to block his shot. Those things happen, but it seemed like he needed someone to blame—and that someone was me. I did feel bad for him. I know it hurt, but more than that, it took him quite a while to get back to normal with that ankle.

One more thing about this period. Travel.

I had lived near and worked in New York City in the seventies. And much of my travel for my company took me there in the eighties and nineties. I spent a lot of time there and was familiar with at least lower and Midtown Manhattan. I had an idea how rough the place could be. But I also knew how exciting and fun it could be. I was convinced that (as the song goes) if you can make your way there, you can make your way anywhere. No other town—at least where English is widely

---

[3] Pax says I'm too hard on myself about this. I appreciate it, and that's his opinion. But I disagree.

spoken—would be nearly as intimidating.

Because of that, I took the boys to New York once every year or two. We saw the Mets play several times, saw several Broadway plays and a lot of sites. Whenever we went, I laid out a challenge—first to Matt and then a few years later to Pax. The best example was my challenge to Pax about two days before a Mets game to get us to the game and back. I told him that cabs are not always available and comparably quite expensive. So, our mode of transport was to be subway.

We were staying in Midtown Manhattan, and the game was in Queens at Shea Stadium—probably a thirty- to forty-five-minute subway ride. So, for a kid in his early teens, it wasn't necessarily a slam dunk.

But both guys met the challenges well. I don't think either one of them failed one.

We also traveled each year to the beach. Generally, in those days, we were content to pick a different beach each year and rent a house on the beach. It couldn't be across any streets—had to be on the beach. We had a great time exploring different beaches for a while and finding new things. Eventually, though, we settled on the Outer Banks for a long while.

I try not to speak for them on important issues, but I think I'm reasonably safe in saying that the boys and I loved those trips. Even after the beach, we'd hit Busch Gardens on the way home—just to be sure we had a last good time before returning to work and school.

About the only issue we had during these trips was Matt's dim opinion of the business trips I sometimes was asked to take during those beach vacations. My company and its parent had filed for bankruptcy protection in 1991 over a series of contracts it had committed to in the seventies (before I came on to the scene—just to be clear). Because the company's business was subject to intense federal regulation, the proceedings were doubly complicated. And I happened to be well versed about the problem contracts—thus, I had a central role for both my company and its parent's proceedings.

So, for two or three years in a row, the company would send a plane to fetch me from the beach, take me to the parent board meeting in Delaware (later Virginia), and fly me back that evening. It might sound glamorous to some. But those who travel a lot know it was anything but glamorous. I had to get out of vacation mode and into work mode in the middle of a week's vacation. Not easily done.

To my surprise, Matt's was the most vocal and strident voice in objection to this practice. Of course, he didn't have anyone but me to object to, so I would listen and respond, but I always went. I was complimented by his outrage. It let me know that he thought his old man worked hard and was deserving of some uninterrupted vacation time with his family. Kinda neat when the kid acts out of a desire to protect his dad.


## Looking Back


This period from about 1991 through 1996 or 1997 was very busy. I spent even more time out of town tending to my company's legal issues—and there were plenty of those. I remember having occasion to ask my secretary to count my nights away from home over the preceding twelve months. I don't remember exactly what the count was, but I do remember it was almost twice the number of the next most-traveled senior manager.

The only reason I minded the travel was because of the effect on my sons. I was weathering the wear and tear well. But I was worried about my boys.

I think that's in large measure why I began to get more emotional about things than I had been. Don't get me wrong. I was very emotional about losing Carol as it happened and for months afterward—no question. But now I was seeing things in my sons that somehow were more related to my parenting—or, better put, my parenting shortcomings. I'm sure part of it was guilt at having to be gone so much and wondering whether I was striking the right balance between career and kids.

But part of it was also knowing I'd missed some things. That hit me especially hard with Pax. He was so young when we lost his mother, and over time, I came to seriously wonder whether I'd let him down. I've never quite put my finger on it, but I've never felt like I did as good a job as I should have.

There were other reasons for the emotion too. Frankly, the romantic interest opened me up quite a bit. Having spent a decade convinced all that was behind me, and then to experience someone caring for me in that way, resulted in a whole new way of thinking about myself. And to be honest, I think it "tenderized" me to some extent. Perhaps it was a combination of that and age.

Finally, there was the realization forced upon me by Matt's departure for college that these kids who a short while ago seemed so totally dependent on me were leaving soon. All parents want to see their kids grow, mature, and take on the world as adults. But most, if not all, parents also feel a sense of loss. And it's not simply a loss of their own time or a marker for their own life. There is a sense that the five- or ten- or sixteen-year-old kid who still lives inside this young adult is now covered up by everything that adult has learned and no longer needs you. Proud parent, but a bit sad too.

I might be overstating all this—but only slightly, I think. I've already observed that after Carol was diagnosed (and certainly after she died), I was more easily reduced to tears by things I never thought would affect me that way. And I certainly had moments with the boys when it would get to me. Those usually occurred when there was a confluence of things in my mind—the departure of one kid and then the other only a short time after, the knowledge (or at least my suspicion) that Pax had probably been left to figure out some things that I could (or might) have helped him with.

Then, along with the realization that the day-to-day work of raising those boys was almost finished, came the pride in who and what they were. Damn. That alone was enough for me to get emotional. I remember how scared (and how sure) I was that I was going to screw things up. To have lived through that fear and to see the young guys developing the way they have was and is overwhelming. So my emotional spells were really the result of a combination of things: the loss of Carol, the knowledge that she hadn't enjoyed the journey with me in raising these two boys, and the sense of satisfaction at how they turned out.

I've often been complimented about what good guys my sons are. My response has always been the same. Good parents are made by good kids who make the right choices. Don't get me wrong. There are plenty of good parents out there who do the right things just like me, or even better than I did, but whose kids get off track and make some bad choices. I know some of my peers raised kids who sometimes made bad choices about drugs or something equally serious. It doesn't mean those parents weren't good ones. But I was lucky to have two sons who kept most of their mistakes minimal both in number and magnitude.

# 14
# Launching the Boys
# (1997–2015)

Before I knew it, Matt had graduated from college and was headed for law school. He chose Washington and Lee in Virginia—a very good school—one he called a "big boy" law school to differentiate it from the state school I attended.

Meanwhile, it became Pax's turn to leave for school. This departure didn't sneak up on me like Matt's did. I had already been through one kid leaving, and here was the last. Damn. He and I had grown somewhat closer after Matt had left the house, and now he was going to be gone. I didn't have any easier time leaving Pax at school than I had with Matt.

The house was empty, and that wasn't healthy for a single guy in his forties. Although it might have freed me up a bit more for dating (I had broken up with the first love interest by then), it was hardly a worthwhile trade-off. I didn't fall into terrible habits, but I do remember plenty of lonely evenings.

I focused primarily on work again. By then I had become general counsel of my company and was enjoying my job for the first time in quite a while. The company had emerged from bankruptcy with essentially new management, and it was a time for building and strengthening. All that was fun.

Among the three of us, things went along uneventfully for several years. Then, around the year 2000, we all fell in love. Yep. All three of us—at the same time. Well, almost the same time.

After his second year of law school, Matt was invited to

work as a paid intern with a firm in Pittsburgh. He went up there alone, found his own apartment, signed a lease, moved in, and began working. Though I was proud he could and wanted to do all those things for himself, it also made me feel unneeded in a strange sort of way. I don't think I ever saw that apartment.

But I did see what came next. As I recall, Matt first raised the subject of a girl he had met in Pittsburgh during a routine check-in phone call with me in midsummer. He told me she was interning at the same law firm and that they'd taken a dislike to each other at first. Obviously, that didn't last long. He told me he'd been out with her a few times and things were going well.

Now, like any father, I thought (at least in some ways) my sons were decent catches for any young lady. But Matt had never spoken to me about liking a girl or dating. I knew he generally had his eye on one classmate in high school, and he did pass through Charleston with a young lady when he was in undergrad school, but I could tell neither of those was serious.

This was different. I don't think Matt told me so, but I could tell that there was potential with this girl. My suspicions and hopes were confirmed later that year when Pax and I met Matt at a cabin I'd rented in a state park. We had begun to supplement our beach vacations with an autumn weekend in the mountains. Matt told us he was in the process of having a ring made and planned to ask this girl to marry him soon. Pax and I were happy for him and understandably eager to meet this girl who was going to be asked to join our family. We did just that only a few months later. By the way, Matt did pop the question, and she said yes.

So, now Matt's departure was nearly complete. I'd always told each son that when he committed to a woman, she would and should supplant me and his brother as the most important people in his life. That person would be the one each would share everything with. All parents know that day will come, and most are happy when it arrives. But there's a bit of a sense of loss as well. More on the wedding and marriage later.

Meanwhile, Pax continued to prove me wrong about being so vulnerable because he'd lost his mother at such a young age. As he came into his twenties, Pax grew up quite a bit, in large part because he fell in love. Pax had met his future wife while still in high school, and I think they both knew quickly that the attraction between them was both mutual and special. But they both had some growing up to do. So, Pax and his girl had a few years of uncertainty between them, but by the time he was a junior or senior in college, they were well committed to each other.

At about that time, I'd undergone a couple of major events. I retired from my company on my fiftieth birthday. The parent company was being sold, and it was clear to me that the guys in charge of the purchaser knew very little about the business of my company, which was highly regulated. It was also clear that these guys were going to centralize decision making at the higher levels of the new parent's management.

I wasn't thrilled at the idea of working for them, so I looked to my financial advisor to see generally what my situation was. I was surprised to learn that I could retire and enjoy essentially the same standard of living. Hmm. So, I did just that.

After all those years of pressure, beginning with Carol's diagnosis, through a very complicated bankruptcy, and followed by a major change of management, I was now free to spend my time as I wished. I took a year off just to sit back and relax. I can't tell you how many people commented to me how differently I looked and acted. Apparently, the tension of the previous eighteen years had been more obvious than I'd been aware. Now that it was gone, the comments came rolling in. "You look so young!" "You're so laid back now." "You used to intimidate me, but now…" Jeez.

The second event was that I fell in love for the second time in my life. I'd met her just ten days or so before I retired from my company. In fact, one of my assistant general counsels had interviewed her and wanted to hire her. I was asked to meet her and give final approval to the hire, which I did. At the time, I thought, "Very attractive girl, but unfortunately almost eighteen years younger than me. Too bad."

I didn't think too much of it until a couple of months later when I was invited back for the departmental summer picnic. She and I began talking and spent most of the afternoon together. I simply took it as the new kid on the block seeking some pointers from the grizzled retiree. But we met again a couple of months later at another guy's retirement party and again spent most of our time talking.

I knew I was attracted but never dreamed she would be— at least not until I spoke with my former secretary a few days later. She observed that we'd spent a lot of time talking and suggested that the attraction was mutual. I didn't buy it until a month or so later during the holidays. Pax and I were at a bar when she walked in, saw us, and joined us. We couldn't have spent more than ten minutes talking when she got up to use the restroom. Pax looked at me and said something like, "What the hell?"

After he lectured me about my inability to read what was going on, I told him to hit the restroom when she returned. He did. I asked her out, and she said yes. Damn.

We dated for over four years. But in the end, she wanted children, and I didn't. I wanted to want them—for her sake, if for no other reason—but at fifty-plus years of age, I couldn't be sure I could be the "hands on, get out with them and play" dad I always thought myself to be. The parting was very friendly. She now lives in the Midwest with a beautiful little seven-year-old girl, and we communicate for one week every April (our birthdays are only four days apart). Couldn't be happier for her.

Matt's wedding was eleven days after 9/11. Despite the timing, the wedding was a happy event. Matt and his bride made sure to pay homage to the victims of 9/11. In fact, Pax made a short speech just before the ceremony that hit just the right tone. In short, they made it a happy few days for everyone—especially at the reception. It was a very informal affair at his new wife's childhood home.

Pax's wedding was a few years later—another very nice event. Like Matt's reception, Pax's was held outside at a nice park with plenty of sunshine. And it lasted quite a while. It had been a long time since I'd stayed up partying late enough to see dawn, but I saw it the morning after that wedding.

So, both boys were launched from home—both on their own, each commencing work on his marriage and family. One might have thought my job was done. In a sense, it was. But any parent will tell you that you never stop being a parent—no matter what. A parent never stops cheering for his or her child or wanting the best for them, regardless of the child's age or circumstance.

I've been on my own for the most part since Pax was married. I did marry again. But we realized pretty quickly that we'd made a mistake. So, we divorced in pretty short order and went our separate ways.

I'm happy though. I see my grandkids often and stay engaged with folks at work and socially. Maybe I'll even marry again, though it seems unlikely. We'll see.

# 15
# Three Man Game
# (1985–2015)

No one could read these pages and fail to see how important basketball has been to my sons and me. I taught them what I knew of the game. We learned more about it together. We followed the Celtics in the eighties, watched Jordan in his prime convince us one by one that he was probably the best to ever play the game, and we watched many college games together, especially during March Madness each year. Even now when we're not together, we sometimes have a three-way text session with full commentary on and reaction to the game we're watching. But most importantly, we played the game.

Our special rules of the game for three guys were well developed and perfectly suited to our respective abilities.

The hours we spent playing were countless. The games were always hard-fought and competitive. We each won our share, and we all got miffed from time to time. But we also developed a bond among us that will always endure. I think the last time we played was sometime in the early 2000s, when I was in my fifties.

The meaning that our game held for us became clearer when the boys and I were in the process of forming a company as a vehicle for some joint investments. I had begun work with a private-equity group, and although we're not extremely well off, we did have occasion to put this company together. We struggled for a couple of weeks to come up with an appropriate name until Matt came up with "Three Man Game" as the name for our company.

It resonated immediately with all of us. It was clearly descriptive of an activity we'd developed and enjoyed for over twenty years. But it also served well as a fitting name for our jointly owned company and as a metaphor for our preceding twenty years together—sort of an "us against the world" thing.

No one else appreciates it like we do.

# Looking Back and Where We Stand Now (2015–2016)

So, having reached the thirty-year mark since Carol's passing, I've picked up this writing again and completed it. Part one, from my standpoint, had to be written—for me, if for no one else. I think it was a therapeutic exercise in 2005 that helped me get past some of the sadness and tragedy of our loss. I had gained happiness by the time I started it and was in a much healthier frame of mind than I had been at times before then. In fact, although it didn't work out in the end, I had fallen in love by then and could have committed totally had things been different.

Part two was not as necessary for me to write. And it may not be very useful or entertaining to anyone else. For those reasons, it didn't come to me as easily as most of part one did. But that's OK. Maybe the point of it is that we made it—or are making it. By that, I mean we're each building lives but with room for all of us in those lives.

Both sons have embarked on careers—Matt is in law (though I think he'll run a business one day), and Pax earned an MBA degree. He too should be running an enterprise before he's finished. They're both smart in ways I never dreamed of. More importantly, they're good, honorable guys. Both are teachers and coaches. I couldn't be prouder.

We still spend time together. In fact, we work on some matters together—more as peers, though, than as father and sons. We finally made it to an NCAA tournament session this year and plan on another next year. I'm still a parent, but I'm much more a friend now. My youngest will tell me from time to time that I can still act "parental" with my advice, and he's right. But I do try to keep it to a minimum.

My two daughters-in-law make my sons happy and are good for them. For that alone, I love them. But beyond that, they are both extraordinary young women, each in her own way. Both run a tight ship at home and are the mainstay of my sons and their kids. Both are great partners for the two men my sons have become.

Between them, they've produced six grandkids (five boys, now twelve, eleven, nine, six, and a few months, and a four-year-old girl). I have a relationship with each child and enjoy them all.

I know I run the risk in all the "Looking Back" sections of coming off as more than a little preachy. It's not intended to be so—rather it's simply a part of my nature from time to time to state what might be obvious to many. Well, here's another "looking back" point I think is worth making: when one undergoes a tragedy, the temptation might be to conclude that no one quite understands or that no one else has been through tragedy like yours.

That conclusion is simply wrongheaded, and the temptation to come to that conclusion should be resisted. The fact is, everyone has bad things happen, and none of those things are any less tragic than what might have happened to you. What makes my (or your) tragedy so terrible is that it happened to me (or you). And just because someone might not appear to be suffering today, don't assume that person has never suffered tragedy. Unless a person talks about it (and many don't), you may never know what happened. Just as importantly, even if those persons haven't yet suffered, don't assume they won't. Any one of us could be days or even minutes away from a terrible diagnosis or an automobile accident that could take away our health or even someone (or maybe several someones) very important to us. Just do the best you can with what you have—and don't worry about the other guy.

Although this is the close of part two, the lives together of my sons, my daughters-in-law, and now my grandkids are far from over. I plan to be around for quite a long time to watch them all and to enjoy my own life as new opportunities and books develop. Maybe one day, folks will hear from me again. I just hope someone gets something out of all this.

Cheers.

# Postscript

Time works on a person. Even though one might hold strong convictions about his or her conduct and thoughts, time can erode those convictions—perhaps not completely, but some.

I have always taken comfort in knowing that Carol loved (loves) me and I her and that she knew those things. But after almost thirty years, one begins to wonder. Have I romanticized things? Have I convinced myself of something that isn't as true or as strong as I thought? Like everyone else, I'm human. So, these thoughts occurred to me increasingly as time passed.

In the fall of 2014, I got an e-mail from a woman who was probably Carol's best friend ever. She and Carol had begun kindergarten together and went through elementary school in tandem. Even though they attended different high schools, they remained close and spoke often. When Carol and I moved back to our hometown (both times), she and Carol always reconnected and found time for each other.

Her e-mail came to me in the latter part of 2014. She simply wanted to make contact and say hello and maybe get together to catch up. We did just that. I knew our conversation would likely focus on Carol, our memories of her, and events.

And I was right. We shared many memories—some laughing, some crying—about what one might expect.

But then she told me something I'd never heard before. She had received a call from Carol a good two or three weeks before she passed. Carol was in the hospital, and we were trying new chemo drugs, hoping for the best.

Their conversation was pleasant and nothing terribly special until the end. Carol told her that this call would likely be the last time they spoke. Carol wanted to tell her friend some things. One of those things was that she was so thankful she had found and experienced real romantic love in her life. Carol told her friend that she loved me and that she knew I loved her.

I'm tempted to conclude that God does things like this on occasion—bringing someone into one's life to deliver a message or for some other purpose. But maybe it was mere coincidence. Who knows? The important thing for me is the reaffirmation of what I'd thought for almost thirty years. That was special and will remain so to me until my turn comes—and I hope even after that.

I hope everyone gets such a gift at some point in life.

Again, cheers.

www.ingramcontent.com/pod-product-compliance
Lightning Source LLC
Chambersburg PA
CBHW060304050426
42448CB00009B/1749